RELEASED BY THE
DETROIT PUBLIC LIBRARY

Parliamentary Procedure
Essential Principles

Parliamentary Procedure Essential Principles

M. STANLEY RYAN

CORNWALL BOOKS
New York • London • Toronto

Cornwall Books
440 Forsgate Drive
Cranbury, N.J. 08512

Cornwall Books
25 Sicilian Avenue
London WC1A 2QH, England

Cornwall Books
2133 Royal Windsor Drive
Unit 1
Mississauga, Ontario L5J 1K5, Canada

Library of Congress Cataloging in Publication Data

Ryan, M. Stanley.
Parliamentary procedure.

Includes index.
1. Parliamentary practice. I. Title.
JF515.R93 1985 060.4′2 83-45012
ISBN 0-8453-4771-3

Printed in the United States of America

Contents

Preface

Parliamentary law? We have to be careful of our interpretation of the word *law.* Not exactly incorrect, the term can be misleading. It should be used only in its widest possible sense; our commonly accepted concept is too restrictive. There is no parliamentary law, adopted by any legislative assembly, which must be obeyed by all deliberative assemblies. *Parliamentary procedure* is the preferred term to use. It is more descriptive and, therefore, more meaningful.

The use of Parliamentary procedures is relatively new in democratic societies. It began about eight hundred years ago when the English adopted a technique for operating their representative government. When this technique was developed, it became known as parliamentary procedure, that is, the procedures needed to operate a parliament.

America inherited the spirit of parliamentary procedure but not all its form. When the Constitution was adopted, Thomas Jefferson used the customs of the British Parliament to draw up the rules of procedure for the United States House of Representatives. Jefferson tempered these rules mainly because of his experience in the House of Burgesses and the Continental Congress. The procedures of the House of Representatives were used as a guide by

General Henry Martyn Robert in drawing up his rules of order for use by the general public.

General Robert was born on May 2, 1837. He was commissioned in the United States Army (Engineers) in 1857. His first book, *Rules of Order,* was published February 19, 1876. It became an immediate success. In 1915, he published an enlarged version titled *Robert's Rules of Order Revised* (ROR). This book sold well over 2.5 million copies and was considered in many quarters to be the standard manual on the subject in the United States. General Robert died in 1923 at the age of eighty-six.

Two other books, little known but very important, were written by Robert in the later years of his life. *Parliamentary Practice,* which Robert intended as an introduction to parliamentary law, was published in 1921. *Parliamentary Law,* published in 1923, the year of his death, was written as a textbook rather than a manual. Both books went out of print and were not available until they were recently republished, at the behest of the National Association of Parliamentarians, as bicentennial editions of Robert's work.

Robert's Rules of Order Newly Revised (RONR) was written by Sarah Corbin Robert, daughter-in-law of General Robert, with the assistance of Henry M. Robert III, James W. Cleary, and William J. Evans. The original RONR was published in 1970. A revised edition was published in 1981. This revised edition is said to be in complete harmony with the previously published works of General Robert. It has gained general acceptance among deliberative assemblies and has largely supplanted the original edition. It is the authority on which this textbook is based.

The course in parliamentary procedures, as outlined in this textbook, is designed to help the individual to quickly master the essentials needed to participate effectively as a member of a deliberative assembly. If called on to preside, he or she will be able to conduct a meeting with the poise and confidence which comes from knowing that established rules and customs are being observed.

The text is arranged so as to lead the student progressively through a basic course of training in the subject and, at the same time, inculcate an awareness of the intricacies of parliamentary law. Basic considerations, such as the customary pattern of formality to be used by members in addressing each other or the chair, types of rules governing a deliberative assembly, officers and their duties, the proper order of business, and various types of meetings are given in the forefront of the text. This is followed by an outline of the thirteen motions with relative rank among themselves, that is, these motions are placed in an orderly arrangement in which one of higher rank is given priority for consideration by the assembly over one of lower rank when both are pending. Following these motions is a list of the most commonly used incidental motions with rules that pertain to each. The concluding portion of the text is devoted to topics that are also important in helping the student to understand the essentials of parliamentary procedure: boards and committees, voting, nominations and elections, content of bylaws, and conventions.

Motions may be characterized as the foundation stones on which the structure of parliamentary law is built. Their importance cannot be overemphasized. The basic course consists largely of a thorough study of motions, with the in-depth analysis of each including the following issues:

- The relative rank of those having rank
- The definition and purpose of use of each motion
- The rules governing each, which should be committed to memory
- The form used in making the motion
- The precedence a motion takes over other motions
- Motions to which a motion yields
- Motions to which a motion may be applied

- Motions which may be applied to a motion
- Other applicable characteristics

A careful study of this textbook will help the student develop the skills necessary to become a knowledgeable chairman and a qualified, professional parliamentarian.

Parliamentary Procedure
Essential Principles

1

Basic Principles

1 The Deliberative Assembly

(RONR, p. 1)

1.1 An organized society consists of a group of individuals who have joined together in a concerted effort to attain a common objective. Ideally, the deliberative assembly of such a group should consist of its entire membership, meeting together to pursue matters of mutual interest. However, as this is practically impossible for any except the smallest of organizations, (perhaps a dozen or so members) it leaves the society no alternative other than to establish a quorum comprised of a smaller group. (See *quorum*.) This smaller group is authorized, by means of the established quorum, to legally conduct business in the name of the entire organization. Members are free to act according to their judgment. They know that the vote of each member has equal weight and that the majority usually prevails. They know also that mere disagreement with a decision of the group is not in itself sufficient cause for withdrawal.

Principle of Decision

1.2 According to common parliamentary law, the basic principle in deciding any resolution or motion brought before a deliberative assembly is a majority vote of that body. However, there are exceptions worth noting:

- When the bylaws require a vote to be more than that of a majority, as in the case of amending the bylaws
- When a motion has the effect of suspending a rule of order
- When the parliamentary right of a member is abridged or infringed on
- When a motion is made to amend something previously adopted

Types of Deliberative Assembly

1.3 The principle types of deliberative assemblies are:

Assembly of an organized society
Convention
Legislative body
Mass meetings

Boards, as opposed to committees, are recognized as a type of assembly. Committees are always regarded as detached groups subordinate to an assembly.

Assembly of an Organized Society

1.4 The assembly of an organized society is limited to persons who are recorded on the rolls of the society as voting members in good standing and who attend a properly called, legal meeting with an established quorum present.

1.5 Provision is usually made to hold meetings at stated intervals, such as weekly, monthly, quarterly, or sometimes even annually.

1.6 Each meeting of such an organization normally constitutes a separate session. (See Chapter 7.)

The Convention

1.7 A convention is an assembly of delegates chosen, normally for one session only, as representatives of constituent units or subdivisions of a much larger body. (See Conventions.)

1.8 The delegates sit and act in the name of the larger body. They must hold proper credentials as voting members and be certified to the convention by the convention's credentials committee.

1.9 The adjournment of the convention dissolves the assembly; unfinished business cannot be carried over to a future convention.

The Legislative Body

1.10 A constitutionally established, public, law-making body of representatives chosen by the electorate for a fixed term of office.

1.11 Its sessions may last for months, during which time it may meet daily. Its members are paid to devote their full time to its work.

1.12 Members can be legally compelled to attend the legislature's meetings.

Mass Meeting

1.13 A mass meeting is a meeting of an unorganized group which is announced as open to anyone interested in a particular problem or purpose as defined by the sponsors of the meeting.

1.14 A large attendance is not an essential feature of the mass meeting, although it may usually be desired.

1.15 A series of meetings held for the purpose of organizing a society are in the nature of mass meetings until the society has been formed.

(For a detailed exposition on the conduct of a mass meeting for the purpose of organizing a society see "Dramatization of the Conduct of Business in a Mass Meeting"—7.26–32, pp. 56–63.)

Minimum Officers

1.16 Two officers are the minimum number needed to conduct business in a deliberative assembly: One, who presides, is known as the presiding officer. The other, known as the secretary, makes a written record of what was done; this is usually called the minutes of the meeting.

Quorum

1.17 A quorum is the minimum number of members who must be present at a meeting of a deliberative assembly for business to be transacted. The chief purpose of a quorum is to prevent a totally unrepresentative minority from meeting and transacting business in the name of the entire organization. According to RONR, a quorum is defined as a *number* "which should approximate the largest number that can be depended on to attend except in very bad weather or other extremely unfavorable conditions" (RONR, pp. 16, 17). Although this *number* may be determined on the basis of a certain percentage of the membership, it is not advisable to express a quorum in terms of a percent of the membership inasmuch as the total membership may fluctuate sufficiently to create an imbalance which may not be known at the time of the meeting.

1.18 A provision in the bylaws should specify the number of members required to constitute a quorum. Lacking such a provision, a quorum would be a majority of the membership of the entire organization. Some bylaws impose additional requirements such as: "Sixteen members, provided two are elected officers, shall constitute a quorum."

1.19 A quorum is needed only for the transaction of business. It applies to the number present, not the number present and voting.

Pattern of Formality

1.20 The president, or chief officer of an organized society, is addressed as "Mr. President" or "Madam President."

1.21 The vice-president, when actually occupying the chair, is also addressed as "Mr. President" or "Madam President" unless the president is on the platform and some confusion would be created as to whom the remarks were intended.

1.22 As a general rule, the president should never be addressed by the personal pronoun "you." If additional terms are needed to refer to the presiding officer, members should speak of him or her as "the chair." "Mr. President, do I understand the chair to say. . . ?"

1.23 Members should try to avoid mentioning another member's name whenever possible. For example, "Mr. President, may I ask the member to explain the purpose of his remarks?" or "I hope the gentleman who spoke last will think of the consequences. . . ."

1.24 The chair (presiding officer) should never use the personal pronoun "I." He or she should always use the third person. Examples: "The chair rules that. . . ," or "Your president is pleased to report. . . ." He or she should also avoid the use of a member's name. "Did the member vote on the prevailing side?"

2 Decorum in Debate

(RONR, p. 331)

2.1 Decorum may be defined as an observance of the rules of ethical conduct by one who regards himself as a member of a class of people whom, for want of a better term, we label "polite society." This includes propriety of manners, speech, and dress and other attitudes of behavior and deportment which bespeak an innate sense of refinement.

Formality

2.2 The pattern of formality outlined in 1.20–1.24 lends itself to the development of decorum in debate. Observance of these customs enables a neophyte to learn quickly the standards and rules of conduct expected of a member of the assembly.

Courtesy

2.3 *Courtesy* is a byword that should always be kept in mind. It is of greatest importance that the courtesies be observed even in small discussion groups.

Principles of Debate

2.4 Certain principles should prevail in every discussion.

2.5 Confine remarks to the merits of the question immediately pending. (There are a few instances in which discussion can include a motion not immediately pending. Familiarize yourself with the rules that permit you to discuss these motions; they are exceptions.)

2.6 Avoid personalities. It is not in order to reflect on acts of the assembly or on the acts of any member.

2.7 Refer to officers by their official titles.

2.8 Confine discussion to the measure under debate. Do not attack or question the motives of an opponent. It is the question, not the man, that is the subject of debate.

2.9 Questions should always be directed to the chairman or, through him, to the speaker to be questioned. Members do not directly address each other in a deliberative assembly. Communication is through the chairman.

2.10 A member, if speaking in debate, should immediately release the floor and take his seat if the presiding officer rises to speak on a pertinent matter. The member remains seated until the chair again recognizes him or her as having the floor.

2.11 The maker of a motion cannot speak against the motion; however, the member who seconded the motion is not so restricted. The seconder merely agrees that the motion should come before the assembly, and the act of seconding the motion is not indicative of whether he or she is in favor or against the motion when it is presented to the assembly for a decision.

2.12 During debate, a member, may request general consent to read from a paper for the purpose of substantiating the member's remarks. If another member objects, even after the member who made the request has begun reading, he or she cannot continue without permission being granted through a vote by the assembly.

2.13 During debate, or while business such as voting is being transacted, it is out of order for a member to create a disturbance by talking or moving about the room.

Duties of the Chairman

2.14 Duties of the chairman are many and varied. one of the chief responsibilities of a presiding officer is to guard against any breach of decorum by a member during debate. This is considered a paramount duty.

2.15 The following examples illustrate the action to be taken and manner in which the chair should handle given situations should they arise during debate:

2.16 To participate in debate, the presiding officer must relinquish the chair (a) to the vice-president (or the senior vice-president) who has not spoken to the question and has indicated he has no desire to speak, (b) to some other qualified member who, presumably, meets with the approval of the assembly, or (c) If some other member is nominated by a member of the assembly, the chair's choice becomes a nominee and the matter is decided by vote.

2.17 When a member is called to order by the chairman for disciplinary reasons, the chair should insist that the member take his seat until the question of order is decided. He cannot proceed without the permission of the assembly. If, in spite of repeated warnings by the chair, the member persist in continuing the breach of etiquette in debate, the chair can name the offender. This amounts to preferring charges and should be used only under extreme circumstances.

2.18 In case of objectionable words, the secretary should record them, so that there will be evidence if disciplinary action is to be taken.

2.19 The chair should never permit debate to begin before the question has been properly placed before the assembly. Five steps are required: 1) Member rises and addresses the chair. 2) The chair recognizes the member, who is now said to "have the floor." 3) Member having the floor makes a motion, "I move that . . ." (*not,* "I make a motion that . . ."). 4) Another member, without rising, seconds the motion, "I second the motion," or simply says, "Second." 5) The chair states the question, "It is moved and seconded that . . . (repeating the motion). Are you ready for the question?" or, "Is there any debate?"

The question may now be debated under the rules governing debate. Debate must be germane to the pending question. The maker of the motion is entitled to speak first. The chair should alternate the floor when possible between members speaking in favor of and those speaking against the question. Each member may speak twice but cannot make a second speech if another member who has not spoken desires the floor. Each speech is limited to ten minutes unless permission is granted by the assembly or the rule is modified by a special rule of order.

3 Rules of an Assembly or Organization

(RONR, p. 7)

Basic Considerations

3.1 Each organization has certain requirements peculiar to itself—no two are exactly alike. These differences must be taken into account when drafting a set of rules to govern its operation. For example, there are organizations whose membership is comprised solely of individuals. There are others that have only established businesses as unit members and still others whose membership reflects a combination of both individuals and established businesses.

3.2 While certain rules are necessary to establish the basic structure of these organizations, such rules are, of necessity, limited in their application due to the diverse nature and composition of these organizations. Because of the prevalence of this situation, each organization should feel free to adopt any rules, even those which deviate from the accepted principles of parliamentary law, provided that, in the process of adopting them, the organization conforms to parliamentary procedure or its own existing rules.

Types of Rules

3.3 The types of rules that may be formally adopted are as follows:

Corporate charter
Constitution and/or bylaws
Special rules of order
Rules of order
Standing rules

Corporate Charter

3.4 A legal instrument which sets forth the name and object of the society and other information needed to incorporate under the laws of a particular state.

3.5 The principal advantage of the charter is that the officers and members are protected from personal liability under obligations that may be incurred by the organization.

3.6 The charter should be drafted by a lawyer and must be processed in accordance with the legal procedure for incorporation in the state (or under federal law if applicable).

Constitution and Bylaws

3.7 A constitution is a document embodying the principles and containing certain rules under which members of an organization consent to be governed. It was formerly a common practice, when organizing a club or society, to divide the rules governing the organization into two parts, one being called the constitution and the other the bylaws. The purpose of this division was to assign to the constitution the more important rules and to make these rules more difficult to amend than those assigned to the bylaws. However, with the passage of time, it became apparent there was nothing to be gained by such a division. It is now a common practice, and one recommended by RONR, that all rules of this kind be combined into a single instrument, usually called the bylaws.

3.8 Bylaws serve as a fundamental instrument establishing an unincorporated society. They prescribe how the society functions and include all rules the society considers so important that (1) they cannot be changed without previous notice to members and the vote of a specified large majority, such as a two-thirds vote, and (2) they cannot be suspended, with the exception of clauses that provide for their own suspension under specified conditions.

3.9 The number of articles in the bylaws are usually determined by the size and activities of the organization. The following list is typical of those found in the average unincorporated society:

Name of the organization
Its object or purpose
Membership
Officers and their duties
Meetings
Executive Board and/or Executive Committee
Committees
Parliamentary Authority
Amendment

(A convenient way to remember these nine articles listed above is to use the acronym *NO-MOM-EC-PA*.)

3.10 Bylaws supersede all other rules of a society except the corporate charter, if there is one. They have a direct bearing on the rights of members in the organization, whether present or absent from an assembly.

Special Rules of Order

3.11 Special rules of order supersede any rules in the parliamentary authority with which they may conflict.

3.12 These rules are usually adopted in the form of resolutions, but when they are printed the enacting words "*Resolved,* That" are dropped.

3.13 Any special rule of order should be adopted separately from the bylaws and should be printed in the same booklet with, but under a heading separate from the bylaws.

3.14 For the adoption or amendment of special rules of order, previous notice and a two-thirds vote, or without notice, a vote of the majority of the entire membership.

3.15 For the suspension of a special rule of order, a two-thirds vote is required except for a rule protecting a minority of less than one-third of those voting. For example, a special rule of order requiring a three-fourths vote in order to sell property, protects a minority of one-fourth of those voting, therefore such a rule cannot be suspended by a two-thirds vote. RONR states, "No rule protecting a minority of any particular size can be suspended in the face of a negative vote as large as a minority protected by the rule" (RONR, p. 223).

3.16 Special rules of order are easily distinguished from standing rules in that special rules always have a parliamentary connotation, whereas standing rules are purely administrative in nature.

Rules of Order

3.17 Refers to written rules of parliamentary procedure formally adopted by an assembly or organization. These rules relate to the orderly transaction of business in meetings and to the duties of officers in that connection.

3.18 Rules of order derive their proper substance largely from the general nature of the parliamentary process rather than from the concerns of a particular assembly. Consequently, there is little reason why most of these rules should not be the same in all ordinary societies.

3.19 The method by which an ordinary society provides itself with suitable rules of order is to include in its bylaws a provision that a specified and generally accepted manual on parliamentary law shall be the organization's authority.

3.20 The organization may then adopt only such special rules of order that it finds it needs to supplement or modify the rules contained in the manual which has been adopted.

3.21 It is unwise for an assembly or society to attempt to function without formally adopting a recognized parliamentary authority.

3.22 When a society has adopted a particular parliamentary manual as its authority, the rules contained in that manual are binding upon it in all cases where they are not inconsistent with the bylaws or any special rules of order of the body.

3.23 Rules of order can be suspended by a two-thirds vote except a rule protecting a minority of less than one-third of those voting. The fundamental rights of each member are inviolable. A rule requiring previous notice to amend rules of order cannot be suspended even by unanimous vote, for its purpose is to protect the absentees and they have not consented to its suspension.

Standing Rules

3.24 Standing rules are related to the details of administration rather than to parliamentary procedure. They are adopted if and when needed.

3.25 They can be changed upon the same conditions as any ordinary act of the society.

3.26 They may be printed under a separate heading in the booklet containing the bylaws, and when so printed, any enacting words such as "*Resolved,* That" should be dropped.

3.27 A standing rule can be adopted by a majority vote without previous notice. Such a rule, remains in effect until rescinded or amended; however, it does not bind future sessions if a majority desires to suspend it temporarily for the duration of a particular session.

3.28 Standing rules in conventions differ from ordinary standing rules in some respects. Standing rules pertaining to conventions are discussed in Chapter 20.

4 Officers and Their Duties

(RONR, p. 375)

Elected Officers

4.1 The following are considered to be the elected officers of an organization:

President
Vice-president(s)
Secretary
Treasurer
Directors, if any

Elected or Appointed Officers

4.2 The following may be elected or appointed as prescribed by the organization's bylaws:

Historian
Librarian
Curator
Chaplain
Sergeant-at-arms

Appointed Officers

4.3 The following may be appointed as prescribed by the organization's bylaws:

Executive Secretary
Parliamentarian

Duties of the President

4.4 The following is a brief outline of the duties of the president:

- Call the meeting to order and preside.
- Announce business in proper order.
- Recognize members entitled to the floor.
- State and put all questions coming before the assembly.
- Announce results of votes distinctly.
- Enforce rules of debate and decorum.
- Expedite business.
- Decide questions of order.
- Answer questions relating to parliamentary procedure.
- Have at hand bylaws, parliamentary authority, lists of standing and special committees and their chairmen.
- Have an agenda.
- Entertain all legitimate appeals.
- Refrain from entering into discussion.

Rights of the President

4.5 The rights of the president are enumerated as follows:

- To vote when the vote is by ballot
- To vote last on roll call
- To vote to make or break a tie vote

- To vacate the chair if he or she desires to debate the question before the assembly

Duties of the Vice-President

4.6 The duties of the vice-president are delineated as follows:

- Preside in the absence of the president.
- Assume the authority of the president in the event of an emergency.
- Assume the office of president in case of the death or resignation of the elected president, unless the bylaws prescribe otherwise.

Duties of the Secretary

4.7 The following duties of the secretary are as outlined below:

- Call the meeting to order in the absence of the president and vice-president and preside until a temporary chairman is elected.
- Keep a record of all proceedings of the organization.
- Keep a complete roll call of the membership of the society.
- Have custody of documents and papers of the organization.
- Have copies of bylaws, lists of committees, agenda, and paper for ballots when required.
- Send a copy of the minutes to the president within a reasonable time.

4.8 Like any other member, the secretary may make motions, second a motion, enter into debate, and vote on questions before the assembly.

Duties of the Treasurer

4.9 The following duties of the treasurer are as outlined below:

- Be custodian of all funds.
- Deposit all moneys in a bank designated by the organization.
- Make a financial report at each meeting.
- Make an annual report which shall be audited.

4.10 The treasurer's report is not "accepted" at each meeting but is filed for audit. The acceptance of the report of the auditing committee carries with it the acceptance of the treasurer's report.

5 Chairmanship

Attributes of a Good Chairman

5.1 The following are among the important attributes of a good chairman:

- Leadership ability
- Understanding of the importance and purpose of parliamentary law
- Knowledge of parliamentary procedures

Leadership Ability

5.2 A good chairman must, of necessity, be a good leader. To keep the business of an assembly moving as rapidly as possible and still have real deliberation, the chairman should use such expressions as: Is there a second? Is there any discussion? Any further discussion?

5.3 He or she must use general consent whenever group opinion appears to be unanimous. "If there are no objections, so and so will be done." After a pause for objections and hearing none, say, "It is so ordered."

5.4 In the conduct of business, the chairman must be vigorous and positive; in the treatment of members, courteous and impersonal.

Understanding Parliamentary Law

5.5 The chairman should have an understanding of parliamentary law and the purpose for which it was developed.

5.6 The four objectives of the rules of order which illustrate this purpose are as follows:

- To maintain decorum
- To ascertain the will of the majority
- To preserve the rights of the minority
- To facilitate the orderly and harmonious transaction of the business of the assembly

Robert's Rules of Order Newly Revised states, American Parliamentary Law is built upon the principle that rights must be respected: Rights of the majority, of the minority, of individuals, of absentees, and rights of all these together.

Knowledge of Parliamentary Procedure

5.7 A chairman should have a working knowledge of parliamentary procedure. This enables a presiding officer to conduct a meeting with the poise and confidence that comes from knowing that established rules and customs are being observed.

5.8 The chairman need not be a parliamentarian; however, he or she should master such basic parliamentary considerations as the order of precedence of commonly used motions.

5.9 The chairman should keep a chart at hand showing the precedence and applicability of motions that are generally used. Figure 5.1 illustrates graphically the ladder of subsidiary motions arranged according to rank with the highest ranking, "Lay on the Table," on top of the page. All motions, after debate for those that are debatable, are put to vote in inverse order of their rank, that is, beginning with the highest if called for and moving downward toward the main motion skipping, of course, any not called for in the list.

This chart can be very useful to the presiding officer. It keeps him/her oriented as to just where he/she is on the "totem pole." This is especially true when diversions occur through the introduction of incidental motions such as a member raising a point of order or rising to a point of information.

The chair is entitled to and can demand that long, involved main motions be presented in written form. (Resolutions are *always* written.) The same is true of amendments or instructions to a committee. All other subsidiaries require only a modicum of writing. A check mark or a brief, understandable note will suffice. For example, a motion to postpone the pending question until 3:00 P.M. and make it a special order for the time stated, can be noted as "3.00 P.M.–SO." on the line opposite "Postpone to a Certain Time."

Since each main motion requires a separate chart, it is advisable to keep several copies on hand.

5.10 The chairman should insist that the assembly recognize the parliamentary necessity of considering one motion at a time.

5.11 The chairman should commit to memory the usual order of business. When no set rule is adopted by a society, the following is in order:

- Reading and Approval of the Minutes
- Reports of Officers, Boards, and Standing Committees
- Reports of Special Committees
- Special Orders

- Unfinished Business and General Orders
- New Business

Voting

5.12 In voting, the chair should present the question to the assembly by saying: "Those in favor say aye. Those opposed say no." The chair must always call for the negative vote, no matter how nearly unanimous the affirmative vote may appear, except in the case of a motion of a complimentary or courtesy nature.

5.13 The chair votes when (1) the vote is by ballot, (2) the vote is by roll call, or (3) in cases where the chair's vote will change the result. For example, the chair might vote yes to break a tie or no to create a tie, thus causing the defeat of a motion. (Note: The chair cannot vote twice, first to make a tie, then to cast the deciding vote.)

5.14 The lone exception to a tie vote defeating a motion is one in which the ruling of the chair is sustained after an appeal against that ruling.

Helpful Hints

5.15 To call a meeting to order, use *ONE* rap of the gavel. The chair uses the gavel only to call a meeting to order and to maintain order.

5.16 Never permit a discussion to start before the question is put before the assembly.

5.17 State each motion clearly so that the members know exactly what business is being considered.

5.18 Be sure to announce not only the result of a vote, but the action to be taken if the vote was in the affirmative and the motion carried.

5.19 The following illustrates the three parts of the chair's response to a vote: "The ayes have it. The motion is carried, and so and so will be done." or "The noes have it. The motion is lost and so and so will not be done." Variations depend on the type of vote taken. If it is a standing vote or a show of hands, the statement would be changed to "The affirmative has it" or "The negative has it," but the three parts enumerated would remain constant. This should be followed by the announcement of the next business in order.

5.20 Never put the negative vote to a complimentary motion, sometimes called a courtesy motion, unless someone objects. (See 5.12 and 20.48.)

5.21 Stand when recognizing a member, putting the question, taking a vote, ruling on a point of order, and in all other instances when addressing the assembly. Be seated when another has the floor during the debate of a question.

5.22 Do not express an opinion or debate a question while occupying the chair. It is the duty of the chair to be impartial and fair.

5.23 Always refer to yourself as "the chair." Do not use the personal pronoun "I."

5.24 The title to use in addressing a member of the assembly is "the member." For example, "Did the member vote on the prevailing side?"

5.25 Study carefully the order of precedence of subsidiary and privileged motions.

5.26 Learn to do by doing. Knowledge, per se, is not sufficient to develop the art of becoming a good chairman.

Fig. 5.1. Chairman's Check Sheet

Lay on the Table: ______________________________

Previous Question: ______________________________

Secondary Amendment: ______________________
____

Primary Amendment: ______________________
____

Limit or Extend Debate: ______________________

Secondary Amendment: ______________________
____

Primary Amendment: ______________________
____

Postpone to a Certain Time: ______________________
____

Secondary Amendment: ______________________
____

Primary Amendment: ______________________
____

Commit or Refer: ______________________________
____

Secondary Amendment: ______________________
____

Amendments: Primary Amendment: ______________________
____

Postpone Indefinitely: ______________________________

Main Motion: ______________________________
____

6 Order of Business

(RONR p. 298)

Agenda

6.1 An agenda, which includes an order of business, may be likened to a letter having three distinct parts: The letter has a beginning, the salutation; a body, the message; and an ending, the complimentary close. An agenda has a beginning, the call to order and opening ceremonies; a body, the business portion; and an ending, the program, announcements, and adjournment.

6.2 In this connection, the important thing to remember is that neither the beginning nor the ending of an agenda require a quorum but the body, or business portion, does. (See Figure 6.1.)

Call to Order

6.3 The meeting is usually called to order by the president saying, "The regular meeting of the (name of organization) will come to order," or simply, "The meeting will come to order."

6.4 One rap of the gavel is considered sufficient; however, we may, in good conscience, exempt from this rule the chairman who opens the meeting of a political convention.

Opening Ceremony

6.5 The call to order is immediately followed by the introduction of guests, if any, then continued with some suitable opening ceremony. In many organizations, the opening ceremony begins when the president calls on one of the members to give the invocation.

6.6 Following the invocation, it is the practice of some organizations to pledge allegiance to the flag of the United States or, in others, to present the colors.

Quorum

6.7 Before proceeding to the business portion of the agenda, the presiding officer checks to make sure that a quorum is present. Business cannot be legally transacted without a quorum.

Reading and Approval of the Minutes

6.8 Having ascertained that a quorum is present, the presiding officer then proceeds to the order of business by directing the secretary to read the minutes of the previous meeting. (See composition of a set of minutes, Figure 6.2.)

6.9 If, for some reason, the minutes of any previous meeting, whether regular or special, have not been read, the secretary should read each separately for approval in chronological order from the date of the last reading, providing that this is one of the organization's regular or adjourned regular meetings. Minutes are not approved at a special meeting.

6.10 At the conclusion of the reading of the minutes, the chair asks if there are any corrections. (It is improper to add "or additions" because any change in the minutes, whether to strike out or add, is a correction.) If there is no response, the chair announces that the minutes are approved as read. If there are corrections, the chair states that the minutes are approved as corrected.

Correspondence

6.11 In some organizations, it is considered appropriate to interpose at this point the reading of any correspondence received since the last meeting. If such is the case, the chair calls on the secretary (or the corresponding secretary if there is one) to read the correspondence.

6.12 Any correspondence requiring action on the part of the assembly can be held in abeyance until the appropriate category in the order of business is reached, usually new business.

Reports of Officers, Boards, and Standing Committees

6.13 Normally officers (with the exception of the treasurer), boards of directors, and chairmen of standing committees do not make reports at each regular meeting. The bylaws usually require that they report at the annual meeting of the organization. However, there are instances when, for special reasons, a report would be in order—if, for example, the chairman of the membership committee, listed in the bylaws as a standing committee, desires to report on the committee's last membership drive.

6.14 A motion to adopt a recommendation or recommendations contained in the report of an officer should be made by a member of the assembly and not by the officer making the report.

6.15 When standing committees report as a group, they are called on in the order in which they are listed in the bylaws.

Treasurer's Report

6.16 After the reading of the minutes, and correspondence if any, the chair follows the successive order of business by calling for the treasurer's report. This report is given for information only and no motion is made to adopt.

6.17 Upon conclusion of the treasurer's report, the chair would ask if there were any questions concerning the report then direct that the report be filed. (For an example of a treasurer's report, see Figure 6.3.)

Reports of Special Committees

6.18 The chair, continuing the next step in the progressive order of business, calls for the report of special committees. Special (ad hoc) committees are called on to report in the order in which they were appointed.

Special Orders

6.19 Having received, and where required, acted on the reports of special committees, the presiding officer considers special orders as the next step in the progressive order of business. Special orders may be created in a number of ways:

- It may result from a provision in the bylaws that a certain matter be considered at a particular meeting, such as the nomination and election of officers.
- It may be brought into being as a result of a main motion, with the maker stipulating that it be made a special order.

- It may emanate from the subsidiary motion to postpone consideration of a pending question until the next meeting and make it a special order for the time stated.
- It may have been adopted as a part of an agenda or program in which there is a specific time set for its consideration in the order of business.
- It may have been pending at the previous meeting when the motion to adjourn was adopted.

6.20 If a special order is created by the motion of a member, it requires a two-thirds vote for adoption.

6.21 With the noteworthy exception of *the special order for a meeting,* which would be taken up immediately following the reading of the minutes, special orders are divided into two general classes: those for which no particular time has been specified, and those fixed to be taken up at a certain time or after a certain event has taken place.

6.22 Those for which no particular time has been specified are simply taken up when nothing interferes with their consideration.

6.23 Those fixed to be taken up at a certain hour automatically interrupt any question that may be pending when the time arrives, with the following exceptions: (1) a special order that was made before the special order now due for consideration, or (2) the privileged motions to raise a question of privilege, to take recess, to adjourn, or to fix the time to which to adjourn.

Unfinished Business and General Orders

6.24 Upon completing consideration of any special orders, the chair moves to the next sequential step in the order of business.

6.25 The chair never asks the assembly if there is any

unfinished business. He or she simply states the first item of business under this heading.

6.26 Unfinished business (not old business) is just what the name implies—it results from adjourning a meeting before completing its order of business.

6.27 General orders are items of business resulting from the postponement of questions that were pending at the previous meeting or as listed under unfinished business and general orders in an approved agenda. In either case, their placement in the agenda of the current meeting requires only a majority vote. General orders are taken up in the order in which they were made. Although unfinished business and general orders both come under the same class of business, unfinished business normally precedes general orders.

6.28 Note that the announcement of unfinished business and general orders is made *only* if the minutes of the previous meeting show there is some business to come up under this heading.

New Business

6.29 Having disposed of unfinished business and general orders, the chair moves to the final class of business in the order of business.

6.30 Members are now at liberty to introduce new items of business in the form of an original main motion or resolution. They may move also, when no motion is pending, to take from the table an item of business that was previously laid on the table.

Ending the Meeting

6.31 There is no rigidly set order of precedence governing this phase of a meeting. Some organizations have made it a custom to discuss informally matters pertaining to the welfare of the organization. This category is generally known as the good of the order. Members may offer constructive criticism which may or may not result in action being taken, depending on the nature and substance of the remarks.

6.32 The organization may conclude its agenda with a program followed by announcements before adjournment.

Program

6.33 The program, for example, although usually placed at or near the end of a meeting, may, if it suits the convenience of the organization, be presented before the minutes are read.

6.34 However, if, for valid reasons, it is necessary to interrupt the prescribed order of business and present the program during the business session, it will be necessary to suspend the rules. This would require either a two-thirds vote or the general consent of the assembly. The latter is usually obtained by the chair asking that the rules be suspended.

6.35 When time for the program has been reached in regular order as set up in the agenda, the chair simply announces this fact.

6.36 At the conclusion of the program, the chair, if thanks are in order (a movie, for example, would be an exception), would briefly thank the speaker or entertainer and then proceed to the matter of making announcements before adjournment. The chair should always make it a point to ask the members of the assembly if anyone has an announcement to make.

Adjournment

6.37 The chair may adjourn the meeting by saying, "If there is no further business to come before the assembly, the chair will adjourn the meeting. . . . [Pause.]. . . The meeting stands adjourned."

6.38 The same can be accomplished by a member making the privileged motion to adjourn. The chair puts this question to vote without debate, and if it is adopted, the assembly adjourns *after* the chair states that the meeting is adjourned.

6.39 The chair, in announcing each progressive step in the order of business should say, "The next business in order is. . . ," *not* "The next order of business is. . . ." Keep in mind there is *only one* order of business. It is permissible to say, "The next item of business is. . . ."

Fig. 6.1. Order of Business

Beginning (No Quorum Needed)
Call to Order . . . . President
Opening Ceremonies: Invocation, Pledge of Allegiance, etc.

Body (Quorum Needed)
1. Reading and Approval of the Minutes
2. Reports of Officers, Boards, and Standing Committees
3. Reports of Special Committees
4. Special Orders
5. Unfinished Business and General Orders
6. New Business

End (No Quorum Needed)
Good of the Order
Program
Announcements
Adjournment

Fig. 6.2. Composition of a Set of Minutes

First Paragraph

1. Record the kind of meeting: (a) regular or adjourned regular, (b) special or adjourned special, or (c) annual.
2. Time, date, and place if not always the same.
3. Name of organization.
4. The fact that the president and secretary were present or the names of their substitutes.
5. Whether the minutes of the previous meeting were read and approved as read or approved as corrected.
6. The presence of a quorum may also be stated.

Body

1. The body of the minutes should contain a separate paragraph for each subject.
2. A convenient way to remember what should be contained in the body of the minutes is as follows:

Group 1. All main motions or motions to bring the question again before the assembly *except* those that are withdrawn.

Group 2. All points of order and appeals, whether sustained or lost.

Group 3. All other motions not lost or withdrawn.

3. The name of the maker of the motion is entered in the minutes but not the seconder unless it is so ordered by the assembly.

Closing Paragraph

1. State the hour of adjournment.
2. Minutes are signed by the secretary. The words "respectfully submitted" are *not* used.

Fig. 6.3. Standard Form for a Treasurer's Report

PARLIAMENTARY LAW CLUB
Center City
Anywhere, U. S. A.

TREASURER'S REPORT

For period beginning January 1, 19__ and ending June 30, 19__.

Balance as of January 1, 19__		$1,166.00
	Receipts	
Dues collected during the period . .	$300.00	
Profit from sale of training material	28.30	
Total receipts		328.30
TOTAL.		$1,494.30
	Disbursements	
Rent for meeting place	$250.00	
Postage	30.00	
Typewriter repair	15.00	
Total disbursements		295.00
Balance in checking account June 30, 19__ . .		$1,199.30
TOTAL.		$1,494.30

Virginia Smith, Treasurer
(Mrs. Robert B.)

7 Types of Meetings

(RONR, p. 70)

Meetings and Sessions

7.1 To obtain a better understanding of the terms *meetings* and *sessions,* it is necessary to compare their definitions. Although these terms are closely interrelated, there are significant differences when they are used in a parliamentary sense.

7.2 A meeting is an assembly of persons who meet together to discuss and act on matters of common interest. In an organization which meets weekly, monthly, or quarterly, each of these meetings is a separate session. However, in the case of a convention lasting several days, the entire series of meetings constitute *one* session. Whenever an adjourned meeting is called, be it regular or special, it is a continuation of the previous meeting, and the two meetings are the *same session.*

7.3 Meetings may be classified under the following headings:

Regular or adjourned regular
Special or adjourned special

Annual meetings
Executive sessions
Mass meetings

Regular Meetings

7.4 The regular meetings of a permanent organization are established in its bylaws. The bylaws should specify the day or days when such periodic meetings occur, for example, "the first and third Wednesdays of each month." The exact hour for the meetings can be made a standing rule.

7.5 During regular business sessions, any business that comes within the purview of the objects stated in the bylaws, can be introduced and acted on. Business beyond the scope of these objects may not be introduced unless, by a two-thirds vote, the assembly agrees to its introduction and consideration.

7.6 The sequence and manner in which business is conducted in the regular meetings of most organizations is usually found in their adopted parliamentary authority.

7.7 *Robert's Rules of Order Newly Revised* states what has come to be regarded as the usual or standard order of business for one meeting sessions of ordinary societies:

- Reading and Approval of the Minutes
- Reports of Officers, Boards, and Standing Committees
- Reports of Special Committees
- Special Orders
- Unfinished Business and General Orders
- New Business.

7.8 Organizations may carry over a main question from one business session to the next, providing the periods between regular business meetings do not exceed three months. Organizations that do not hold regular business sessions as often as quarterly can carry over a main question to their next business session only by referring the question to a committee.

Special Meetings

7.9 A special meeting is a separate session called for some special purpose and held at a time different from that of a regular meeting. Urgent matters requiring attention before the next regular meeting often precipitate such a call.

7.10 The bylaws of the organization should contain a provision stating who is authorized to call a special meeting. The bylaws should also prescribe the length of time required for the proper notification of members. The call should specify the time, place, date, and purpose of the meeting.

7.11 A special meeting should not be confused with *the special order* for a meeting. There are points of similarity, especially when the assembly plans to devote an entire meeting to a consideration of the special order for the meeting. There are fundamental differences, however, that need to be kept in mind.

7.12 Special meetings do not follow the usual order of business. After the call to order and opening ceremonies, if any, the chair reads the purpose of the meeting as specified in the call. The assembly adjourns on completion of the business for which the meeting was called.

7.13 The special order for a meeting simply preempts any other order of business scheduled for the meeting and is taken up immediately after the reading of the minutes. After the special order is disposed of, any other business scheduled, including new business, becomes subject to the sequence prescribed for the standard order of business in a regular meeting.

7.14 The minutes of a regular meeting are not read at a special meeting, but the minutes of a special meeting are read at the next regular meeting.

7.15 If, during a special meeting, it becomes necessary to take action on an important matter not specified in the call, the action taken is not legal until that action has been ratified at the next regular meeting or at another special meeting called for that purpose.

Adjourned Meetings

7.16 If, during a regular or special meeting, the assembly finds itself unable to complete its work, it may provide for an adjourned meeting. This is done by adopting the motion to fix the time to which to adjourn, either as a main motion or a privileged motion. As previously stated, an adjourned meeting is a continuation of the immediately preceding previous meeting, and both meetings constitute the same session.

7.17 An adjourned meeting takes up the order of business where the previous meeting left off or takes up consideration of a question that was postponed. However, the minutes of the previous meeting are read after the call to order and before proceeding to the continuation of the previous meeting and to matters postponed from that meeting.

Annual Meetings

7.18 There are organizations that hold a business session each year for the general membership. Such a session may actually consist of more than one meeting. In such instances, the annual meeting is sometimes called a convention, although, generally speaking, a convention is usually considered an assembly of delegates from constituent units of the organization.

7.19 Local organizations that hold meetings at periodic intervals during the year may, through a provision in the bylaws, designate that one of its regular meetings be the annual meeting. This meeting usually differs from an ordinary business meeting in only one respect: Annual reports of boards, officers, and chairmen of standing committees and the election of new officers are included in the agenda.

7.20 In the case of an organization holding one business meeting a year, a committee is appointed to approve the minutes of the meeting. This committee should be named and the names announced at the beginning of the meeting so that it is fully alerted to its responsibilities.

Executive Sessions

7.21 *Executive session* is another term for secret session, that is, a meeting, or a portion of a meeting, in which the proceedings are secret. Only members and others specially invited are allowed to attend.

7.22 Members can be punished for violating the rule of secrecy, and others are bound not to divulge the nature of any business transacted.

7.23 The motion to go into executive session is under the aegis of a question of privilege. It can be adopted by a majority vote.

7.24 Matters pertaining to discipline, especially trials, should always be held in executive session.

7.25 Minutes of an executive session must be read and acted on only in another executive session.

Mass Meetings

7.26 A mass meeting is a meeting of an unorganized group called to take action on a particular problem or purpose. It is usually open to anyone who is interested and more or less in sympathy with the purpose as expressed in the call.

7.27 The call of the meeting should specify the time, date, and place of the meeting. It should also clearly explain the purpose and, if applicable, who is invited to attend. A statement about the individual(s) sponsoring the call along with the reason for taking this action could prove most helpful in obtaining the response desired.

7.28 The call has a force equivalent to the bylaws of an organized society in that it defines the subject matter within which motions are in order and determines who has the right to participate as members.

7.29 If the call does not specifically state who are invited, those who attend a mass meeting have the same privileges as members of an organized society, that is, the right to make motions, to speak in debate, and to vote.

7.30 The rule that a member of an organized society is permitted, by a two-thirds vote of the assembly, to introduce motions that have no relation to the objects stated in the bylaws of the society, does not apply to a mass meeting. Any attempt to divert the proceedings from the purpose announced in the call is prohibited if the sponsors object. An individual attempting to create such a diversion of purpose is subject to expulsion from the meeting.

7.31 Strong leadership is necessary to insure the success of a mass meeting. *Robert's Rules of Order Newly Revised* states:

Before the meeting, the sponsors should agree on the following:

- whom they prefer for its chairman;
- who shall call the meeting to order and nominate their choice of chairman;
- who shall be nominated for secretary and by whom;
- what rules—if any—shall be proposed for adoption; and
- who shall make the initial talk explaining the purpose of the meeting.

7.32 This premeeting agreement, as well as other principles involving the first meeting of an unorganized group, can best be illustrated by the dramatization of a mass meeting:

[Permission has been obtained from the mayor, the city council, and the police department of Center City, Anywhere, U.S.A., to organize a reserve police force to help combat crime and juvenile delinquency in certain areas of the city. Five civic-minded individuals (Mr. A, B, C, D, and E) have decided to form an association to accomplish this purpose and have issued the call for a meeting. A cover letter giving a detailed explanation of the purpose of the meeting, together with background information regarding the sponsors, was sent out. However, for the sake of brevity, only the official call is included here.]

MR. A [*to Mr. B*]: Looks as if we are going to have a nice crowd. By the way, what is the quorum for this group?

MR. B: We don't have to worry about that—the quorum will be the number present when the meeting is called to order. It represents the entire membership.

MR. A: Well, I'd better get started. [*Leaving the assembled group, he goes to the lectern, and, with one rap of the gavel, gains attention.*] The meeting will come to order. Who will act as chairman? Nominations are in order.

MR. C: I nominate Mr. B.

MR. A: Mr. B has been nominated. Are there further nominations? [*No response.*] If there are no further nominations, the chair declares nominations closed, and Mr. B is designated the chairman of the assembly.

MR. B: [*Mr. B, hereafter designated as chairman, thanks the assembly briefly for the honor of being selected chairman,* then proceeds.] The next business in order is the election of a secretary. Nominations for the office of secretary are now in order.

MR. D: I nominate Mr. E.

CHAIRMAN: Mr. E has been nominated. Are there further nominations for the office of secretary? [*Pause.*]

MR. F: I nominate Mr. G.

CHAIRMAN: Mr. G has been nominated. Are there further nominations? [Pause.] If there are no further nominations, the chair declares nominations closed for the office of secretary.

CHAIRMAN: Those in favor of Mr. E for secretary say aye. Those opposed say no. The ayes have it, and Mr. E is elected secretary.

CHAIRMAN: [*Immediately after the elected secretary has taken his place.*] The secretary will read the call of this meeting.

SECRETARY: [*Standing.*] "Notice is hereby given that a meeting of all persons interested in becoming members of a reserve police force to help combat crime and juvenile delinquency in our city will be held on (date) ________ at (hour) ________ in (place of meeting) ________."

SPONSORS

(Signed) ____________________
Mr. A

____
Mr. B

____
Mr. C

____
Mr. D

____
Mr. E

CHAIRMAN: It is now in order that the object of this meeting be fully explained. Mr. A, will you please come forward and explain the object of this meeting?

MR. A: [*After taking position in front.*]
Mr. Chairman, gentlemen:
As stated in our cover letter which each of you received, we are here to organize a reserve police force to help combat general crime and juvenile delinquency. We hope to be able to put at least one reserve police officer in every ten blocks of the city to augment our regular police force. To qualify as a reserve police officer, the applicant must be an outstanding, civic-minded individual who is willing to accept the responsibility of such an office and serve without pay. Each applicant will be thoroughly investigated before being sworn in and issued the regulation weapon used by our regular police officers.

The police department pamphlet issued to you when you arrived gives you pertinent information on the required training, the time involved, and the arrangements to be made with the police department to receive this training, as well as many other details that need not be discussed here, for these matters have to be resolved on an individual basis. However, I will say this—every effort will be made to see that you receive training without direct interference with your work or business.

We plan also to form an association which will be known as the "Police Reserve Officers of Center City." The purpose of the association will be to provide oversight control over the activities of its members and to develop a liaison relationship with the city's public officials in general and with the police department in particular.

CHAIRMAN: You have just heard the purpose of this meeting explained. This purpose can best be accomplished by a member making a specific proposal in the form of a resolution that can be discussed and disposed of under the rules of parliamentary procedure.

Before asking Mr. D to make this motion, a copy of which each of you has received, the chair will invite your attention to the fact that we have not yet adopted a parliamentary authority.

Robert's Rules of Order Newly Revised is a widely known, authoritative manual, which in the present instance, may be considered persuasive but still does not have the force of a formally adopted parliamentary authority. In order that the deliberations of this assembly follow established rules of procedure, the chair will entertain a motion to formally adopt this manual as our parliamentary authority.

MR. C: I move that this assembly formally adopt *Robert's Rules of Order Newly Revised* as its parliamentary authority.

MR. H: I second the motion.

CHAIRMAN: It has been moved and seconded that this assembly formally adopt *Robert's Rules of Order Newly Revised* as its parliamentary authority. Are you ready for the question? [*No response.*]

As many as are in favor of formally adopting *Robert's Rules of Order Newly Revised* as the parliamentary authority of this assembly, say aye. Those opposed, say no. The ayes have it. The motion is carried, and *Robert's Rules of Order Newly Revised* is the adopted parliamentary authority of the assembly.

Mr. D, please present the resolution that was prepared for this meeting.

MR. D: Mr. Chairman, members of the assembly, the resolution reads as follows:

Whereas, Crime and juvenile delinquency have risen to alarming proportions in Center City; and

Whereas, City officials have requested that the citizens organize a reserve police force as an aid in combating this deplorable situation; therefore, be it

Resolved, That an association to be known as Police Reserve Officers of Center City be formed; and

Resolved, That membership in the association be limited to those who meet the requirements outlined in the police department's pamphlet and who submit their applications for training to become police reserve officers.

Mr. Chairman, I move the adoption of the resolution just read. [*Steps forward and hands the resolution to the chairman.*]

MR. M: [*Without rising.*] Second the motion.

CHAIRMAN: It has been moved and seconded that the resolution just read be adopted. Are you ready for the question?

MR. D: [*Obtaining recognition.*] I came to this meeting hoping that this assembly would be able to accomplish the object set forth in the call. I still have that hope. An affirmative vote on the motion now pending will give us the impetus we need to move forward toward this goal. I would like to see the motion to adopt the resolution carried by a large majority.

MR. H: [*Obtaining recognition.*] I also speak in favor of the resolution. I'm especially interested in the problem of juvenile delinquency. There was a time when juvenile delinquency was considered a big-city problem. In a smaller community such as Center City, a juvenile crime was practically unheard of but now this disease—if one can call it a disease—seems to be spreading everywhere. The other day I picked up an old issue of *Time,* and this is what I read. [*Proceeds to take a printed page from his pocket, obviously torn from the magazine, but is rudely interrupted.*]

INTERRUPTER: What the hell! All this talk about delinquency. I say the shoe is on the other foot. We ought to be investigating police brutality instead of organizing to help them. My boy was kicked and mauled something fierce just because. . . .

CHAIRMAN: Just a minute! I don't know your name, but I do know you are completely out of order. Not only did you fail to obtain recognition from the chair before you spoke, but you have shown yourself to be a disrupting influence. The chair has no recourse other than to ask you to leave immediately. [*Individual leaves hurriedly after noticing three burly sponsors, Messieurs A, C, and D, decending on him from different directions in the hall.*]

Mr. H, you may continue.

MR. H. This is what I read. "Recent statistics proved that the rise in juvenile crime is possibly the most serious aspect of America's crime problem. For example, more than half of all murders, rapes, aggravated assualts, robberies, burglaries, and motor vehicle thefts in the United States are committed by youths ten to seventeen years of age."

CHAIRMAN: Is there further discussion on the motion to adopt the pending question? [*No response.*]

If there is no further discussion, the chair will put the question on adopting the resolution.

Mr. Secretary, please read the resolution in its entirety.

SECRETARY: [*Standing, reads the resolution.*]

CHAIRMAN: The question is on the adoption of the resolution just read. Those in favor, say aye. Those opposed, say no. The ayes have it. The motion is carried and an association to be known as the Association of Police Reserve Officers of Center City is formed. Membership in this association will be limited to those who meet the requirements outlined in the police department's pamphlet and who submit their applications for training to become reserve police officers.

MR. D: [*Obtains recognition.*] I move that a committee of five be appointed by the chair to draft a set of bylaws for our newly formed association and that the committee be instructed to report at an adjourned meeting of this assembly.

MR. H: I second the motion.

CHAIRMAN: It has been moved and seconded that a committee of five be appointed by the chair to draft a set of bylaws for our newly formed association and that the committee be instructed to report at an adjourned meeting of this assembly. Are you ready for the question?

MR. A: [*Obtains recognition*] I am in favor of this motion and would like to see it adopted by a unanimous vote; however, before the vote is taken, I think the assembly should decide when and where to hold an adjourned meeting. I move that when we adjourn, we adjourn to meet in this place at 7:00 P.M. two weeks from tonight.

MEMBER: I second the motion.

CHAIRMAN: It has been moved and seconded that when we adjourn, we adjourn to meet in this place at 7:00 P.M. two weeks from tonight. This motion is not debatable but is amendable as to time and place. Are you ready for the question? [*Pause, no amendments, chair continues.*] Those in favor, say aye. Those opposed, say no. The ayes have it. The motion is carried, and we will have an adjourned meeting in this place at 7:00 P.M. two weeks from tonight. The question now is on the adoption of the motion "that a committee of five be appointed by the chair to draft a set of bylaws for our newly formed association and that the committee be instructed to report at the adjourned meeting of this assembly." Is there any debate? [*No response.*] Those in favor, say aye. Those opposed, say no. The ayes have it. The motion is carried, and a committee of five will be appointed by the chair for this purpose.

[*Carefully scanning the assembly, then looking directly at each appointee, the chair continues.*] Mr. A, Mr. C, Mr. D, Mr. G, and Mr. H are appointed members of the committee to draft a set of bylaws for our newly formed association and report at the next meeting, which will be an adjourned meeting held at 7:00 P.M. in this place two weeks from tonight.

Is there any further business to come before the assembly? [*No response.*]

Are there any announcements? [*No response.*]

The chair is curious. How many members feel that they can meet the police department's requirements to become a trainee and are planning to sign an application for admission to the program. Those who plan to do so, please rise. [*Counts forty-eight.*]

Forty-eight out of fifty-five is not a bad percentage at all; in fact, it is a very good percentage. The chair would like to remind you to bring your signed application with you to our next meeting.

If there is no further business to come before the assembly, the chair will declare this meeting adjourned. [*Pause.*]

The meeting stands adjourned until the next meeting, which will be an adjourned meeting held at 7:00 P.M. in this place two weeks from tonight.

2

Motions

8 General Classification of Motions

(RONR, p. 48)

8.1 Motions are classified into five general classes: main, (incidental main), subsidiary, privileged, incidental, and motions that bring the question again before the assembly. Main motions are themselves divided into two types: original main motions and incidental main motions.

8.2 An original main motion brings a new, substantive question before the assembly on a subject which requires action by the assembly.

8.3 An incidental main motion is a convenient parliamentary aid, generally procedural in nature and usually expressed by a parliamentary term, used to assist the assembly in the conduct of its business. For example, each of the five lowest ranking subsidiary motions becomes an incidental main motion if moved when no business is pending. The privileged motions to recess, to adjourn, and to fix the time to which to adjourn, also have incidental main motions as their counterparts. The relationship of an incidental main motion to the business of the assembly reflects either on its past, present, or future action:

- Past action—A motion to amend bylaws
- Present action—A motion to take recess, made when no business is pending
- Future action—A motion to adjourn, say at 3:00 P.M.

8.4 Subsidiary motions are applied to main motions and certain other motions for the purpose of *modifying* them, *delaying action* on them, or otherwise *disposing* of them. (ROR, page 23)

8.5 Privileged motions have no relationship to the pending question, but are of such importance as to require them to take precedence over all other motions, with certain specified exceptions. (ROR, page 23)

8.6 An incidental motion arises out of another question which is pending and must be decided before the pending question, or other business, is taken up. (ROR, page 23)

8.7 RONR originated a class of motions now known as motions that bring a question again before the assembly and defined them as motions that serve the function described by the name of the class. Motions that fit into this category are as follows:

Amend Something Previously Adopted
Rescind
Discharge a Committee
Reconsider
Take from the Table

(For detailed information, see 14.1.)

9 Main Motion

(RONR, p. 82)

9.1 A main motion brings before an assembly any particular subject on which action by the assembly is desired.

Rules

9.2 The rules governing this motion are as follows:

- It is not in order when another has the floor.
- It requires recognition.
- It requires a second.
- It is debatable.
- It is amendable
- It requires a majority vote except: (a) when the bylaws prescribe more than a majority vote, (b) when the motion has the effect of suspending a rule of order or the parliamentary right of a member, or (c) when the motion has the effect of changing something already adopted.
- Both affirmative and negative votes can usually be reconsidered. However, in changing something already adopted, the incidental main motions to Rescind or to

Amend Something Previously Adopted are sometimes used. When these motions are used, only the negative vote, that is, a vote in which the negative side prevails, can be reconsidered. Discharge a committee, also an incidental main motion, is another instance in which only the negative vote can be reconsidered.

Form

9.3. "Mr. Chairman, I move that. . . ." or "Mr. Chairman, I move the adoption of the following resolution: *Resolved,* That. . . ."

Precedence

9.4 This motion takes precedence over nothing.

It yields to all privileged, incidental, and subsidiary motions.

Application

9.5 A main motion can be applied to no other motion. All subsidiary motions and applicable incidental motions can be applied to main motions.

Other Characteristics

9.6 A main motion may be made *only* when there is no other business before the assembly except one made under the aegis of a Question of Privilege.

9.7 No motion is in order that conflicts with the charter, bylaws, special rules of order, standing rules, or previously adopted resolutions of the assembly.

9.8 A motion to refrain from doing something should not be made. For example, it is incorrect to move "that our delegates be given no instructions." The same result can be accomplished by adopting no motion at all.

9.9 It is preferable to avoid a motion containing a negative statement.

Wrong: "I move that our chapter go on record as not being in favor of changing the date of the convention."

Right: "I move that our chapter go on record as being unalterably opposed to changing the date of the convention."

9.10 Note that voting down a resolution that would express a particular opinion is not the same as adopting a motion expressing the opposite opinion. If the motion is voted down, no opinion has been expressed.

9.11 A main motion, when postponed to a certain time or laid on the table, carries with it all pending subsidiary motions. If a main motion is referred to a committee, it carries with it only pending amendments.

9.12 A motion to adopt the report of a standing committee on a subject *not* referred to the committee is an original main motion.

9.13 A main motion is in the possession of the assembly *after* it has been stated by the chair.

9.14 The chair may require that all main motions, amendments, and instructions to a committee be in writing.

9.15 The maker of a motion can vote against his own motion but not speak against it.

10 Resolutions

(RONR, p. 87)

10.1 A resolution is simply a main motion in written form with a format dictated by an established custom. It usually consists of one or more clauses of a preamble followed by one or more enacting clauses. The preamble outlines the background or reason for making the motion, and the enacting clause, or clauses, is the motion itself.

Preamble

10.2 A preamble need not be used merely for the sake of form. The chief purpose of its use is to provide little-known background information or to make certain reasons for action a matter of record.

10.3 A preamble traditionally follows a specific form:

- Each "Whereas" begins with a capital "W" and is followed by a comma.
- The first word after each "Whereas" begins with a capital letter despite the comma preceding it.
- Each "Whereas" begins a separate paragraph and the

thought is expressed in a single sentence, which ends in a semicolon.

- The next to the last paragraph of a preamble should contain the word "and" after the semicolon with no punctuation following the word. (This is optional for the preceding paragraphs.)
- The last paragraph should close with a semicolon after which a connecting expression such as "therefore, be it" or "now, therefore be it" is sometimes added. No punctuation should follow this connecting expression, and it should always be placed at the end of the preamble paragraph, never at the beginning of the resolving paragraph.
- No periods are used throughout the preamble.

10.4 Resolutions may be introduced without a preamble. In such instances, an introductory phrase is all that is needed. The following is an example of a simple resolution without a preamble:

I move that we adopt the following resolution:

Resolved, That it is the sense of this assembly that the United States shall maintain an adequate standing army.

Resolving Paragraphs

10.5 The resolving paragraphs of a resolution follow the traditional pattern:

- Anent the word *Resolved:* when printed, it should be italicized; when written, it should be underlined.
- *Resolved* is always followed by a comma.
- The word *That,* which follows, should begin with a capital letter despite the comma that precedes it.
- Each resolving paragraph may end in a period, although this is not recommended, or close with a semicolon followed by the word *and,* at least in the next to the last paragraph.

Four Types of Resolutions

10.6 There are four types of resolutions:

- Those not having any preamble at all (see example in 10.4).
- Those with a preamble of only one "whereas."
- Those having a preamble of two or more "whereases."
- Those that have one or more enacting paragraphs.

10.7 The following examples cover all conceivable types of resolutions:

With a preamble of one "whereas":

Mr. Chairman, I move that we adopt the following resolution:

Whereas, No parliamentary law, authority, or dictionary recognizes the expression *Chairperson;* therefore, be it

Resolved, That the organizations and parliamentarians of the National Association of Parliamentarians *must* use the term *Chairman* and should encourage the use of this term in all organizations where they have influence.

With a preamble of more than one "whereas":

Mr. Chairman, I move the adoption of the following resolution:

Whereas, Since time immemorial the terms "*Mister* Chairman" or "*Madam* Chairman" have always been used to differentiate between sexes; and

Whereas, Further effort toward sex differentiation is redundant and contrived; be it

Resolved, That the organizations and parliamentarians of the National Association of Parliamentarians *must* use the term *Chairman* and should encourage the use of this term instead of *Chairperson* in all organizations where they have influence.

With more than one "Resolved":

Mr. Chairman, I move that we adopt the following resolution:

Whereas, *Robert's Rules of Order Newly Revised* provides that the word *Chairman* be used to designate presiding officers who are not presidents or vice-presidents; therefore, be it

Resolved, That the organizations and parliamentarians of the National Association of Parliamentarians *must* use the term *Chairman* and should encourage the use of this term instead of *Chairperson* in all organizations where they have influence; and be it further

Resolved, That all NAP members should habitually stress the principle that the word *Chairman* belongs to the title of the office the same as the title of president or secretary.

11 Subsidiary Motions

(RONR, p. 52)

11.1 Subsidiary motions may well be termed the working motions in parliamentary law. They serve to modify, delay, or dispose of the main motion and certain other motions to which they may be applied.

Order of Precedence

11.2 The order of precedence (pre *ce'* dence) of subsidiary motions *must* be learned. They are listed here in sequential order of rank from the lowest to the highest:

Postpone Indefinitely
Amend
Commit or Refer
Postpone to a Certain Time
Limit (or Extend) Debate
Previous Question
Lay on the Table

Mnemonics

11.3 A few mnemonic notes will simplify the learning process:

- All subsidiary motions require recognition and a second.
- The three highest are *not debatable.*
- The lowest and the two highest are *not amendable.*
- There are three that require a two-thirds vote: (1) postpone to a definite time, when made a special order for the time stated, (2) limit (or extend) debate, and (3) the previous question.
- The motion to reconsider the vote may be made with the following exceptions: a motion to postpone indefinitely can only be reconsidered in the event of an affirmative vote; the previous question can be reconsidered only if no action (vote) is taken under the order; a motion to lay on the table may *not be reconsidered.*

POSTPONE INDEFINITELY (RONR, p. 105)

11.4 The purpose of this motion is to dispose of a question without voting on the motion itself.

Rules

11.5 The following rules govern the motion to postpone indefinitely:

- It is out of order when another has the floor.
- It requires recognition.
- It requires a second.
- It is debatable.
- It is *not* amendable.

- It requires a majority vote.
- *Only* the *affirmative* vote may be reconsidered.

Form

11.6 "Mr. Chairman, I move to postpone the question indefinitely."

Precedence

11.7 The motion to postpone indefinitely takes precedence over nothing except the main question.

It yields to all other subsidiary motions, to all privileged motions, and to all applicable incidental motions.

Application

11.8 This motion can be applied only to the main question. If adopted, it kills (for the session) the question to which it was applied. If lost, it cannot be renewed.

Other Characteristics

11.9 A motion to postpone indefinitely permits a member who has exhausted his right to debate the main question another opportunity to debate its merits. It opens the main question to debate.

11.10 This motion is sometimes used by strategists to test their strength on a motion they oppose.

11.12 If a motion is referred to a committee while postpone indefinitely is pending, the motion to postpone indefinitely is ignored.

11.13 If the main motion is postponed to a definite time or laid on the table, the motion to postpone indefinitely continues to adhere to the main motion and is not ignored. It goes forward with the postponed question and remains for consideration when the main question is returned for consideration at the end of its postponement. The same procedure applies when the main motion is laid on the table.

AMEND (RONR, p. 108)

11.14 The purpose of the motion to amend is to modify a motion, which has already been presented, in such a manner that it will be more satisfactory to the members of the assembly.

Rules

11.15 The following rules govern the motion to amend:

- It is out of order when another has the floor.
- It requires recognition.
- It requires a second.
- It is debatable, except when the motion to be amended is undebatable.
- It is amendable (primary amendment only, a secondary amendment cannot be amended).
- It requires a majority vote.
- The vote may be reconsidered.

Forms

11.16 "I move to amend by adding. . . ."

"I move to amend by inserting the word . . . before the word. . . ."

"I move to amend by striking out the word . . . and inserting the word. . . ."

"I move to amend by striking out the word (or the words or paragraph). . . ."

"I move to substitute for the pending resolution the following resolution: *Resolved,* That. . . ."

Precedence

11.17 If applied to a main motion, the motion to amend takes precedence over the main motion and the motion to postpone indefinitely.

11.18 If applied to other than a main motion, it takes precedence over the motion it proposes to amend.

11.19 The motion to amend *yields* to any other motion that would take precedence over the motion to be amended, except that, if applied to an amendment, it would not yield to a motion to divide that amendment or to consider seriatim.

11.20 The motion to amend *yields* to higher ranking subsidiary motions, all privileged motions, and incidental motions incidental to itself. However, it does not yield to a motion to divide the main question or to consider the main question seriatim.

11.21 It also *yields* to motions to limit or extend the limits of debate or for the Previous Question when they are applied to it and it *yields* to motions incidental to itself.

Application

11.22 A motion to amend may be applied to any main motion and any motion having a variable. For example, it can be applied to change the duration of a proposed recess.

11.23 The motions that may be applied to a motion to amend are: amend, modify debate, previous question, withdraw, and consider seriatim.

Other Characteristics

11.24 According to *RONR,* there are three methods of amending, or modifying, a motion:

- To *insert* or to *add:* (a) to *insert words* or, if they are placed at the end of the sentence or passage being amended, to *add words,* (b) to insert a paragraph or, if it is placed at the end, to *add a paragraph.*
- To *strike out:* (a) to *strike out consecutive words,* or (b) to *strike out a paragraph.*
- The third method of amending provides an indivisible combination of striking out and inserting and has the following forms: (a) to *strike out and insert,* which applies to consecutive words, and (b) to *substitute,* which, in effect, is to strike out a paragraph, or the entire text of a main motion or resolution, and insert another (RONR, p. 112).

11.25 Motions to amend by striking out and inserting, when applied to consecutive words, can be further amended only by striking out; however, the words proposed to be inserted may be amended in any of the three forms just given.

11.26 The term *substitute* is never applied to anything less than a complete paragraph of one or more sentences.

Classification

11.27 Amendments are classified as follows:

- An amendment of the first degree; however, *primary amendment* is the preferred term.
- An amendment of the second degree; however, *secondary amendment* is the preferred term.

11.28 A primary amendment is an amendment to a motion stated by the chair and must be germane to that motion, that is, have a direct bearing on the subject matter of the motion which it seeks to modify.

11.29 A secondary amendment is an amendment to the primary amendment and must also be germane to the primary amendment.

Improper Amendments

11.30 No amendment may be made which:

- Would not be germane to the motion it seeks to amend.
- Would have the same effect as a negative vote on the pending question.
- Would make the question, as amended, identical with, or contrary to, one previously decided.
- Would change an amendment into another form (Example: "strike out" to "strike out and insert").
- Would convert a parliamentary motion from one form to another (Example: postpone to a definite time to postpone indefinitely).

Creating Blanks

11.31 Creating a blank is an incidental motion. Filling blanks is somewhat like amending in that the device is used for making changes in a main motion or a primary amendment.

Rules

11.32 The following rules govern the motion to create a blank:

- It is out of order when another has the floor.
- It requires recognition.

- It requires a second.
- It is *not* debatable.
- It is *not* amendable.
- It requires a majority vote.
- The vote may *not* be reconsidered.

Form

11.33 A member may offer a main motion or an amendment containing a blank: "Mr. Chairman, I move that we donate *blank* number of dollars to the American Red Cross."

11.34 A member may move that a blank be created by striking out. "Mr. Chairman, I move to create a blank by striking out 'one hundred dollars' from the motion that our Club donate one hundred dollars to the American Red Cross." If this motion to strike out is adopted, the part struck out automatically becomes one of the proposals for filling the blank.

11.35 The chair may suggest creating a blank by general consent. The term "general consent" is considered to be more precise terminology than "unanimous consent." The word "unanimous" can be misleading for there are instances when there is no unanimous agreement but the small minority elects to keep silent rather than to expose its views. The chair might say, "Unless there is an objection a blank will be created as to the amount of money to be donated and the chair will entertain suggestions from the assembly for filling this blank."

Filling Blanks

11.36 Any member may suggest—without a second—a way of filling a blank. No member may suggest more than one proposal except by general consent. The number of alternatives which may be proposed is unlimited. Each proposal is debatable and each is voted on separately. Voting continues until one receives a majority vote.

11.37 Filling a blank with *names* is handled in the same manner as nominations from the floor for an elective office. Each nominee is voted upon in the order proposed until enough to fill the blank have received a majority vote. If the number suggested is the same as the number required, the blank can be filled by unanimous consent.

11.38 Whenever a logical order is apparent, a blank involving *money* should be filled by voting on the proposed entries so that the one least likely to be acceptable is voted on first.

11.39 In voting to *spend money,* the amounts should be arranged and voted on in the order from the *highest to the lowest.* In voting to *sell,* the amounts being considered should be arranged and voted on in order from the *smallest sum to the largest.*

11.40 In filling a blank with *places, dates,* or *numbers,* a choice can be made as follows:

- Vote as in filling a blank with names.
- Vote, as with money, beginning with the least popular choice.
- If there is no clear-cut reason, vote on the largest number, the longest time, the most distant date, and so on.

COMMIT OR REFER (RONR, p. 140)

11.41 The purpose of the motion to commit or refer is to refer a pending question to a small group or committee so that the question may be carefully investigated and put in better condition for consideration by the assembly.

11.42 The three variations to the motion to commit permits the entire assembly to deliberate with the freedom of a committee, that is, with no limit on the number of times a member can speak to the question or its amendments. These variations are committee of the whole, quasi committee of the whole, and informal consideration. Detailed information concerning these three types of committees is found in Chapter 16, which deals with committees.

Rules

11.43 The following rules govern the motion to commit:

- It is not in order when another has the floor.
- It requires recognition.
- It requires a second
- It is debatable. (Debate is limited to the propriety of committing the main question and the suitability of the committee. It also permits giving instructions to the committee.)
- It is amendable. (Amendments are limited to proposing a change of committee, adding instructions, or specifying or modifying the method of appointment.)
- It requires a majority vote.
- The vote may be reconsidered if the committee has not begun consideration of the question.

Form

11.44 There are four essential elements needed in the appointment of an ordinary committee: (1) its composition, (2) how it should be appointed, (3) what it is to do, and (4) when it should report. Thus:

Mr. Chairman, I move that a committee of three be appointed by the chair to investigate the possibility of purchasing the land adjacent to our clubhouse and to report at the next meeting of this assembly.

Precedence

11.45 A motion to commit or refer takes precedence over:

- Main motion and lower ranking subsidiary motions
- Division of the question
- Consider by seriatim
- Debatable appeals that do not adhere to the pending question
- Certain debatable appeals in connection with the pending question to which they do adhere. (See RONR, pp. 141–142.)

11.46 The motion to commit or refer yields to higher ranking subsidiary motions, all privileged motions, and applicable incidental motions.

Application

11.47 Motions to commit or refer may be applied to the main motion and adhering amendments, if any; questions of privilege; orders of the day, when pending; and debatable appeals that do not adhere to the pending question.

11.48 Motions that may be applied to motions to commit or refer are amend, limit or extend limits of debate, previous question, withdraw, reconsider.

Other Characteristics

11.49 The power to appoint a committee carries with it the power to appoint the chairman and to fill vacancies.

11.50 If a motion to commit does not include the essential details, it should be completed by amendment or by additional motions immediately after its adoption.

11.51 The first person named by the chair is automatically chairman of the committee. If appointed other than by the chair, the first person named is the temporary chairman, and the committee, usually at its first meeting, names its own chairman.

11.52 If the committee has started work, the matter may be taken from the committee only through the motion to discharge the committee. This requires a two-thirds vote or a majority of the entire membership unless previous notice is given, the committee fails to report as instructed within a given period, or the assembly is considering a partial report of the committee. In these instances, the committee may be discharged by a majority vote.

11.53 It should be noted that in changing a committee one cannot change from one *type* of committee to another through the usual process of amending. (See RONR, pp. 143 and 146.)

POSTPONE TO A CERTAIN TIME
(RONR, p. 150)

11.54 The purpose of a motion to postpone to a certain time is to delay action by postponing the pending question to a definite hour, day, or meeting or after a certain event has taken place.

Rules

11.55 The following rules govern the motion to postpone to a certain time:

- It is out of order when another has the floor.
- It requires recognition.
- It requires a second.

- It is debatable. (Debate is limited as to the propriety of postponement and the suitability of the time.)
- It is amendable. (Amendments are limited as to time. Amendments may also be used to create a special order.)
- It requires a majority vote if a general order is created, a two-thirds vote if a special order is created.
- The vote may be reconsidered.

Form

11.56 "Mr. Chairman, I move to postpone the pending question(s) until the next regular meeting."

"Mr. Chairman, I move to postpone further consideration of this question until 3:00 P.M. and to make it a special order for the time stated."

Precedence

11.57 A motion to postpone to a certain time takes precedence over:

- Main motion and all lower ranking subsidiary motions
- Division of the question
- Consider by seriatim
- Debatable appeals that do not adhere to the pending question
- Certain debatable appeals in connection with the pending question to which they do adhere.

11.58 This motion yields to:

- All higher ranking subsidiary motions
- All privileged motions
- Applicable incidental motions.

Application

11.59 Postpone to a certain time may be applied to the following motions:

- Main motion and lower ranking subsidiary motions which adhere to the main motion
- Directly to debatable appeals that do not adhere to the pending question (see Table 13.3)
- Orders of the day and question of privilege when actually pending
- Reconsideration, when it is in order to postpone the question to be reconsidered

11.60 The motions that may be applied to a motion to postpone to a certain time are:

- Amend
- Limit or Extend Debate
- Previous Question
- Withdraw a Motion
- Reconsider

Other Characteristics

11.61 A question may be postponed to later in the same session, to the next session, or to an adjourned meeting between the present and next regular session.

11.62 A question may be postponed again after being taken up at the time to which it was first postponed.

11.63 A postponed question becomes an order of the day for the time to which it was postponed. It may not be taken up prior to the time set except by (1) reconsidering the vote that established it, or (2) suspending the rules, which requires a two-thirds vote.

11.64 Making the postponed question a special order for a certain time suspends any rules that may interfere with consideration at the time specified except a motion to adjourn or to recess, questions of privilege, special orders made before this special order was made, or *the* special order for a meeting.

11.65 A special order set for a definite meeting without naming the hour comes up under the heading for special orders when that class of business is reached in the order of business.

11.66 A postponed question not made a special order comes up under the heading of general orders, which, although in the same class as unfinished business, normally follows unfinished business. A postponed matter not disposed of before adjournment becomes a part of unfinished business at the next meeting.

11.67 Limitations on the motion to postpone:

- The postponement may be only until the close of the next session if not later than quarterly.
- The motion to postpone may not be applied to an undebatable appeal or to an undebatable motion to reconsider.
- It may not be used to postpone a whole class of business such as reports of officers. Each report must be postponed individually.
- It takes precedence over a debatable appeal only if the appeal does not adhere to the main question.

11.68 A motion to postpone may be renewed after sufficient progress in debate to make it essentially a new question.

LIMIT OR EXTEND LIMITS OF DEBATE (RONR, p. 161)

11.69 The purpose of motions to limit or extend limits of debate is to reduce or increase the number of speeches or the length of time for each speech on the immediately pending question or, if stated as a part of the motion, on a series of pending questions. It may also set a time to end debate.

Rules

11.70 The following rules govern the motion to modify debate:

- It is out of order when another has the floor.
- It requires recognition.
- It requires a second.
- It is *not* debatable.
- It is amendable.
- It requires a two-thirds vote for adoption.
- It may be reconsidered even though partially executed.

Form

11.71 "Mr. Chairman, I move that each speech on the pending question be limited to five minutes."

"Mr. Chairman, I move that each member be limited to one speech on the pending question."

"Mr. Chairman, I move to limit debate on the pending question to twenty minutes."

"Mr. Chairman, I move to extend Mr. Tillotson's time five more minutes."

Precedence

11.72 The motion to limit or extend limits of debate takes precedence over all debatable motions.

It yields to higher ranking subsidiary motions, all privileged motions, and applicable incidental motions.

Application

11.73 A motion to limit or extend the limits of debate may be applied to:

- Any immediately pending debatable motion.
- An entire series of pending debatable motions.
- Any consecutive part of a series of pending debatable motions beginning with the one immediately pending.

11.74 The motions which may be applied to it are amend, previous question (to stop amendments), and withdraw.

Other Characteristics

11.75 An amendment to the motion to limit or extend the limits of debate requires a majority vote. However, the motion itself, inasmuch as it affects the parliamentary right of members, requires a two-thirds vote for adoption. After adoption, any change in limitation or extension, either through the process of amending something previously adopted or through reconsideration (without debate) of the unexecuted portion of the order, would require the same vote that it took to adopt the motion originally, that is, a two-thirds vote.

11.76 The order to limit debate applies only to the immediately pending question if it does not specifically include other questions that were pending at the time it was made.

11.77 The order limiting debate is exhausted when votes have been taken on all questions on which it was ordered or at the close of the session in which it was adopted.

Motions to postpone definitely or lay on the table the pending question(s) remain under the order if again taken up in the same session. However, if the pending question is referred to a committee, the order is exhausted even if the committee returns the question to the assembly in the same session.

11.78 An order *limiting debate* applies not only to the questions on which it was ordered, but also to any debatable motions made subsequently while the order is in force. An order *extending debate* affects only the motion(s) pending at the time it is made.

11.79 If the order does specify a time for closing debate and taking the vote, the pending question(s) may not be referred to a committee or postponed definitely.

11.80 The motion to limit debate is classified as an incidental main motion if made while no motion is pending. When made under such condition it becomes debatable, but still requires a two-thirds vote for adoption.

PREVIOUS QUESTION (RONR, p. 166)

11.81 The object of this motion is to close debate and/or further amendments to the pending question or questions.

Rules

11.82 The rules governing this motion are these:

- It is out of order when another has the floor.
- It requires recognition.
- It requires a second.
- It is *not* debatable.
- It is *not* amendable.
- It requires a two-thirds vote.

- It may be reconsidered *only* if no vote has been taken under the order.

Form

11.83 "I move the previous question."

"I move the previous question on the motion to commit and the amendment."

"I move the previous question on all pending questions."

Precedence

11.84 This motion takes precedence over (1) all debatable and amendable motions to which it is applied, and (2) the subsidiary motion to modify debate.

It yields to all privileged motions, applicable incidental motions, and the motion to lay on the table.

Application

11.85 When not qualified, the previous question applies only to the immediately pending question—the last question stated by the chair. When qualified, it can apply to all debatable or amendable pending questions, or a consecutive part of such a series of debatable or amendable pending questions beginning with the one immediately pending. Unqualified: "I move the previous question." Qualified: "I move the previous question on all pending subsidiary motions." Or "I move the previous question on all pending questions."

11.86 No motion can be applied to a previous question except the motion to reconsider, which may be applied after adoption and before any action is taken under the order.

Other Characteristics

11.87 The previous question, when ordered on a pending resolution, does not apply to the preamble. However, as soon as the preamble is opened by the chair for debate, the previous question may be applied by motion and vote.

11.88 The previous question supersedes any previous order for closing debate at a future time. It also precludes further amendments.

11.89 The motion remains in effect for the session in which it was adopted. Its execution may be interrupted by:

- The main motion, and pending subsidiary motions which adhere, being laid on the table
- a special order set for a certain time
- the adoption of pending subsidiary motions to postpone to a certain time, refer to a committee, or to postpone indefinitely
- the privileged motions—question of privilege, take recess, or adjourn

11.90 If interruption occurs by any means *other than referral* and the question is brought before the assembly again in the *same session,* the order remains in effect.

11.91 The previous question is exhausted when all questions on which it was ordered have been voted upon or when questions under the order are referred to a committee. Even if the questions referred to committee are returned to the assembly at the same meeting, the previous question is no longer in effect.

11.92 The previous question cannot be moved in ordinary committees. However, it may be moved during *infor-*

mal consideration, a form of a committee that is an alternate form of a committee of the whole.

11.93 If a motion to reconsider a vote on the previous question is adopted, it is presumed to have rejected the previous question. This is one instance when the motion to be reconsidered (previous question) need not be again considered, because the order has been overturned by a majority vote.

11.94 A call for the question or "call the question," or "I move we vote now," may be interpreted to mean a call for the previous question made in nonstandard form. The chair may ask if there is an objection to closing debate and amendments even if the "call" had not been seconded. If a member objects or tries to obtain the floor to continue debate, the chair should then ask if there is a second to the "call" if one had not been made. If a second is obtained, he should immediately put the question in the same manner as if the more formal motion of the previous question had been moved and seconded. A two-thirds vote is required to end debate and also end amendments.

LAY ON THE TABLE (RONR, p. 177)

11.95 The purpose of this motion is to lay the pending question aside temporarily.

Rules

11.96 The rules governing this motion are these:

- It is not in order when another has the floor.
- It requires recognition.
- It requires a second.
- It is *not* debatable.
- It is *not* amendable.

- It requires a majority vote.
- The vote may *not* be reconsidered.

Form

11.97 "I move to lay the pending question on the table."

Precedence

11.98 This motion takes precedence over the main motion, all subsidiary motions, any incidental motion pending when it is made.

It yields to all privileged motions and to motions that are incidental to itself.

Application

11.99 The motion to lay on the table can be applied to:

- Main motions.
- Main motions with pending subsidiary motions.
- Orders of the day when they are actually pending as main motions.
- Main motions under the aegis of a question of privilege.
- Debatable appeals that do not adhere to the main motion.
- An immediately pending motion to reconsider, provided that the motion to be reconsidered is also immediately pending. In such a case, the motion to lay on the table carries to the table the motion to be reconsidered and any questions adhering to it.

11.100 No motion may be applied to a motion to lay on the table.

Other Characteristics

11.101 The motion to lay on the table can *never* be qualified in any way. If it is moved to lay a question on the table until a certain time or until after a certain event, it becomes a motion to postpone to a definite time and should be so stated by the chair, providing such a motion is in order according to the rank and precedence of motions.

11.102 The motion to lay on the table cannot be applied to a class of business such as reports of committees or unfinished business. It can only be applied to a question that is actually pending.

11.103 Having been laid on the table, a question remains there until the close of the next business session if not taken up sooner, providing regular business sessions are held at least quarterly. If not taken up by that time, the question dies. This is the prime reason for the frequent misuse of this motion. It should *never* be used with the intent to kill the pending question.

11.104 A question can be taken from the table at a special meeting only if previous notice of such intention is given in the call for the meeting.

11.105 When a motion is laid on the table, it goes to the table with all adhering motions, including the incidental motion "Appeal" if it adheres. When taken from the table, the motion returns in the same manner as it was when laid on the table with one possible exception. The previous question can remain in effect only during the session in which it is ordered; therefore, if the motion to which it was applied is laid on the table then returned to the assembly at the *next* session, the effect of the previous question is exhausted and its control no longer applies.

11.106 If a member has used up his/her allotted time in

debating a question and that question is laid on the table, he/she may not again debate the question if it is taken from the table on the same day. However, if the question is taken from the table on another day, he/she may again debate the question.

11.107 The rules governing the motion to take from the table are exactly the same as those governing the motion to lay on the table.

11.108 The motion to lay on the table, if defeated, may be renewed on the same day if material progress has been made in business or debate or if some unforseen urgent matter develops in the interim period.

12 Privileged Motions

(RONR, p. 56)

12.1 Privileged motions are used to secure immediate action on matters which concern the assembly insofar as they relate to the orderly conduct of business or the comfort and convenience of a member or the group as a whole and on matters of immediate or overriding importance, such as to take recess, to terminate a meeting, or to arrange the time, and sometimes the place, for an adjourned meeting.

12.2 Because of their importance, privileged motions are classified as the elite among the motions having rank. They take rank among themselves at the highest segment of the parliamentary ladder. Higher ranking ones are in order when those of lower rank are pending. They are listed here in order of rank from the *lowest* to the *highest:*

Call for the Orders of the Day
Question of Privilege
To Take Recess
To Adjourn
To Fix the Time to Which to Adjourn

12.3 All privileged motions take precedence over motions of any other class *with the following exceptions:*

- The motion to amend may be applied to the motion to take recess for the purpose of changing the time.
- Amend may also be applied to the motion to fix the time to which to adjourn to change the time and/or place for an adjourned meeting.
- An incidental motion moved while a still higher ranking privileged motion is immediately pending.
- The previous question may be utilized to stop amendments.

12.4 None of the privileged motions are debatable. Other than as just stated, none are amendable.

12.5 There are incidental main motions having the same names as the motions to recess, to adjourn, and to fix the time to which to adjourn. Question of privilege is also handled as a main motion if moved when no motion is pending.

12.6 Privileged motions are also known as privileged questions but should not be confused with questions of privilege. A question of privilege, in itself a privileged motion, is raised by a member when asking permission to make a request that may affect the assembly as a whole, some members of the group, or the individual member making the request.

A question of privilege relating to the assembly as a whole could be one pertaining to the comfort of its members, such as proper ventilation, lighting, heating, and the like. A question of privilege pertaining to some members of the group could entail the adjustment of the public address system so that those in rear of the assembly hall can hear the speaker, and one pertaining to the individual could be simply a request for an individual accommodation, such as permission to remove one's coat. If several questions of privilege are raised simultaneously, the one affecting the greatest number is given precedence over those of lesser numbers and is decided first.

A motion emanating from a question of privilege is treated as any other main motion, that is, it is debatable, amendable, etc. Its privilege lies in the fact that any other business that may have been pending at the time it was introduced is set aside until the motion introduced under the aegis of the question of privilege is acted upon by the assembly.

CALL FOR THE ORDERS OF THE DAY
(RONR, p. 186)

12.7 A call for the orders of the day is a motion to require the assembly to conform to its agenda, or to take up a general or special order when the assigned time has arrived. In effect, it is a demand that the assembly adhere to the proper order of business. This motion is in order and can interrupt another member even though the other member, having received formal recognition from the chair, was given the exclusive right to speak at this time and is said to have the floor.

Rules Governing

12.8 The rules governing this motion are as follows:

- It is in order when another has the floor.
- It does not require recognition.
- It does not require a second.
- It is not debatable.
- It is not amendable.
- If put to a vote, it requires a two-thirds vote in the *negative* to set aside the call.
- The vote may not be reconsidered.

Form

12.9 "I Call for the Orders of the Day."
"I demand the regular order."

Precedence

12.10 This call takes precedence over all other motions except other privileged motions or a motion to suspend the rules relating to the priority of business. A call for the orders of the day yields to the following:

- To all other privileged motions.
- To a motion to suspend the rules relating to the priority of business.
- To any applicable incidental motions.
- To the motion to reconsider or to the calling up of the motion to reconsider previously made, except when a special order must be taken up.

Application

12.11 A call for the orders of the day may be applied (1) when an agenda, program, or schedule of business is being varied from, (2) when a general order that is in order at the time is not taken up, or (3) when the time for considering a special order has arrived or passed. No subsidiary motion may be applied to it.

Other Characteristics

12.12 Although in order when another has the floor, it cannot interrupt a pending question unless a special order is involved.

12.13 The incidental motion to extend the time for consideration of the pending question or, if appropriate, the motion to suspend the rules and take up a desired question may be made in response to a call for the orders of the day. If either one of these motions is made and adopted, its vote offsets the two-thirds negative vote required to keep from returning to the orders of the day. Both motions require a two-thirds vote in the affirmative for adoption.

12.14 Orders of the day cannot, as a whole, be postponed or laid on the table. Such action can be taken only when an individual order of the day is actually pending.

12.15 It is important that business be followed in its prescribed order. This is especially true in conventions; officers, committee members, and delegates must know the approximate time a certain business will come before the assembly.

12.16 As soon as orders of the day that have interrupted the business that was pending are completed, the interrupted business is taken up again at the point where the interruption occurred.

QUESTION OF PRIVILEGE (RONR, p. 191)

12.17 When a situation arises that affects the right and privilege of the assembly or of an individual member, a member can raise a question of privilege. Such a motion demands immediate consideration because of its urgency.

Rules

12.18 The rules governing this motion are as follows:

- It is in order when another has the floor; however, the maker may not interrupt a speaker unless the matter is extremely urgent.
- It does not require recognition.
- It does not require a second.

- It is not debatable.
- It is not amendable.
- It is the chair's responsibility to rule on the admissibility of a question of privilege. This ruling cannot be reconsidered but it may be appealed.
- Inasmuch as no vote is taken on the ruling of the chair on a question of privilege there is no vote to reconsider; however, that ruling may be appealed and the vote on an appeal may be reconsidered.

Form

12.19 "I rise to a question of privilege."

Precedence

12.20 A question of privilege takes precedence over all other motions except the three higher ranking privileged motions. It yields to the three higher ranking privileged motions and to any applicable incidental motion.

Application

12.21 A question of privilege may not be applied to any motion. No subsidiary motion may be applied to it.

Other Characteristics

12.22 Although the raising of a question of privilege is a privileged motion, any motion made as a result of being given permission by the chair is treated as a main motion, with the possible exception of a motion to go into executive session, which, in itself, is a question of privilege.

12.23 The ruling of the chair on a question of privilege may be appealed. The appeal is undebatable, and since it does not adhere to a pending question, none of the subsidiary motions may be applied to it.

12.24 Questions of privilege relating to the assembly take precedence over one that concerns only an individual member.

RECESS (RONR, p. 196)

12.25 The motion to take recess, when adopted, provides a short intermission in the business proceedings of the assembly. After the recess, business is resumed at the exact point in which the interruption occurred. This motion is privileged only when a question is actually pending before the assembly.

Rules

12.26 The rules governing this motion are as follows:

- It is not in order when another has the floor.
- It requires recognition.
- It requires a second.
- It is not debatable.
- It is amendable.
- It requires a majority vote.
- The vote may not be reconsidered.

Form

12.27 "I move to recess for ten minutes."

Precedence

12.28 The motion to take recess takes precedence over (1) all subsidiary motions, (2) privileged motions of lower rank, and (3) incidental motions that are not applicable. It yields to higher ranking privileged motions and applicable incidental motions.

Application

12.29 The motion to recess is not applied to any motion.

The motion to amend may be applied to the motion to recess for the purpose of changing the length of time for recess. The previous question can also be applied to stop amendments.

Other Characteristics

12.30 This motion is *not* privileged if made when no question is pending.

12.31 If a specified time for taking a recess is included as a part of an adopted program or agenda, the chair simply announces the fact and declares the assembly in recess when the specified time arrives. If the chair fails to announce this recess a member may call for the orders of the day.

12.32 A scheduled recess in an adopted agenda has the same status as an order of the day. Since to refuse to proceed to the orders of the day constitutes an interference with the order of business, it requires two-thirds vote to postpone the recess.

ADJOURN (RONR, p. 199)

12.33 This motion is used to close the meeting entirely. It can be made while business is pending providing it is not qualified in any way and providing the time is already established for the assembly to reconvene at a future time. It is also treated as a privileged motion if made when no question is pending.

Rules

12.34 When the motion to adjourn is privileged, the rules governing it are as follows:

- It is not in order when another has the floor or during voting or verifying a vote.

- It requires recognition.
- It requires a second.
- It is not debatable.
- It is not amendable.
- It requires a majority vote.
- The vote may not be reconsidered.

Form

12.35 When the motion is privileged, the form is "I move to adjourn."

12.36 The following forms are examples of the form to use in any of the three instances when this motion is not privileged. The particular form to use depends on whichever is appropriate:

"I move to adjourn at 3:30 P.M."

"I move to adjourn fifteen minutes before the time set for the adjournment of this meeting."

"I move to adjourn sine die" (adjourn without day).

Precedence

12.37 When privileged, the motion to adjourn takes precedence over all motions except the privileged motion to fix the time to which to adjourn.

12.38 It yields to the privileged motion to fix the time to which to adjourn and any incidental motion that may arise and must be disposed of before disposing of the motion to adjourn.

12.39 *Note:* An incidental motion that can wait should not be entertained after a motion to adjourn has been made.

Application

12.40 The motion to adjourn is not applied to any other motion, and no motion may be applied to it.

Other Characteristics

12.41 The motion to adjourn is not privileged if made under the following conditions:

- When the motion is qualified in any way.
- When a time for adjourning is already established.
- When the effect of the motion to adjourn, if adopted, would be to dissolve the assembly with no provisions for another meeting as may be the case at mass meetings and conventions.

12.42 While the privilege motion to adjourn is pending, or even after the motion is adopted but before the chair declares the meeting adjourned, certain matters of overriding importance can be brought to the attention of the assembly for information or necessary action depending on the circumstances surrounding the case. If a particular circumstance requires action before adjournment, the maker of the motion to adjourn can be requested to withdraw his motion.

12.43 The fact that the motion to adjourn is undebatable does not preclude the chair, or any member of the assembly, from taking certain steps such as:

- Making important announcements. The chair conceivably could announce that there will be an executive committee meeting immediately following adjournment.
- Notifying the assembly of urgent business requiring attention. This might take the form of a motion by a member to fix the time and place for an adjourned meeting, if such a matter had not already been decided.
- Making (but not taking up) a motion to reconsider a previous vote. The mere making of the motion is sufficient to suspend action on a motion whose vote it proposes to reconsider. Reconsider can be moved on

any motion whose vote under the rules is reconsiderable but only by one who voted on the prevailing side of the vote proposed to be reconsidered.

- Making the motion to *reconsider and enter on the minutes.* This special form of the motion to *reconsider* outranks the regular motion and is used to forestall reconsideration of a vote on the same day the vote was taken. Reconsider and enter, as it is commonly called, is restricted in its use to motions that dispose of the main question. These motions are: The main question itself, whether carried or lost; an affirmative vote on the subsidiary motion to postpone indefinitely; and a two-thirds negative vote on a question to which an objection to its consideration had been raised. (When the incidental motion, *object to the consideration of the question* is moved, the chair states, "Shall the question be considered?" A two-thirds vote *in the negative* sustains the objection.)
- Giving notice of a motion to be made at the next meeting when the motion requires previous notice. A case in point would be the adoption or amendment of a special order. Motions that have the effect of changing something already adopted or nullifying a previous act by the assembly can also be adopted by a majority instead of a two-thirds vote if previous notice is given.

12.44 If immediately after the chair has declared the assembly adjourned, he learns that a member has been legitimately seeking the floor, he calls the meeting back to order but only for the purpose for which the member had sought the floor.

12.45 The meeting is not adjourned until the chair declares the meeting adjourned. Members should not leave their seats until such declaration is made.

12.46 A meeting can be adjourned without a motion being made if the hour for adjourning has been pre-scheduled. The chair simply announces the fact and declares the meeting adjourned. If it appears there is no further business to come before the assembly, the chair may ask, "Is there further business?" "Are there any announcements?" If there is no response, he states, "Since there is no further business the chair will declare the meeting adjourned. [Pause.] The meeting is adjourned."

12.47 If the assembly has a fixed hour for adjournment, any motion to adjourn, even if made while business is pending, is a main motion and therefore out of order unless the rule fixing the hour is suspended. If the hour of adjournment is prescribed in the bylaws, this rule cannot be suspended.

FIX THE TIME TO WHICH TO ADJOURN (RONR, p. 207)

12.48 The motion to fix the time to which to adjourn is the highest ranking of all privileged motions. It loses its high rank if made when no motion is pending and becomes an incidental main motion subject to the rules governing main motions.

12.49 This motion, when privileged, preempts the current meeting long enough to fix the time, the date, and hour and sometimes the place for the next meeting, which, in parliamentary parlance, is known as an adjourned meeting. It provides for a continuation of the business of the current meeting but has no effect on the time of adjournment of the current meeting. Both meetings (current and adjourned) are considered to be the same session.

Rules

12.50 The rules governing this motion are these:

- It is not in order when another has the floor.

- It requires recognition.
- It requires a second.
- It is not debatable.
- It is amendable, and the amendments are not debatable.
- It requires a majority vote.
- The vote *may* be reconsidered.

Form

12.51 "I move that when we adjourn, we adjourn to meet on the third Wednesday of this month at 8:00 P.M."

Precedence

12.52 This motion takes precedence over all other motions.

It yields to nothing, except that, while it is pending, certain incidental motions such as a point of order may arise and can be disposed of, and the motion to reconsider can be made, but not considered.

(A unique characteristic of the motion to reconsider is the limitation placed on the time it can be made. It can be moved either on the day the vote to which it applies was taken or the next calendar day, not counting legal holidays or a day in which no business is held. Because of this limitation, it enjoys the highest privilege for entry, that is, for the making of the motion, but not for its consideration. For consideration, the motion to reconsider drops beside the rank of the motion whose vote it proposes to reconsider. Thus, if it has been moved to reconsider the vote of a main motion, reconsideration is not in order while any motion of higher rank is pending. In this connection, see also item 3 of paragraph 12.43, also paragraph 14.55.)

Application

12.53 This motion is not applied to any motion. The

motion to amend may be applied to it. The previous question may also be applied to stop amendments.

Other Characteristics

12.54 The date for an adjourned meeting must be set for a time prior to the next regular session.

12.55 As a privileged motion, the motion to fix the time to which to adjourn can be moved even after the assembly has voted to adjourn, provided the chair has not declared the assembly adjourned.

13 Incidental Motions

(RONR, p. 212)

13.1 There is a class of motions which is referred to as incidental motions. RONR states, "As a class, incidental motions deal with questions of procedure arising out of another pending motion, . . . or an item of business." Incidental motions have no rank among themselves, nor in their relationship to any other parliamentary motion. They are primarily concerned with procedural matters that are incidental to the business of the assembly and are logically in order whenever circumstances dictate a need for their use. They must be decided before any other business is introduced.

13.2 Table 13.1 shows some of the incidental motions most frequently used in deliberative assemblies, along with the rules governing their use. The question marks shown on the chart opposite certain incidental motions indicate that there are variables that should be taken into consideration when studying the rules governing that motion. The points that follow undertake an explanation of these variables:

Table 13.1. The Most Frequently Used Incidental Motions and the Rules Governing Their Use

Incidental Motions	Rules					
	Recognition Required	Second Required	Debatable	Amendable	Vote Required	Can Be Reconsidered
• Point of information	No	No	No	No	—	—
• Parliamentary inquiry	No	No	No	No	—	—
• Point of order	No	No	?[a]	No	?	No
• Appeal from the decision of the chair	No	Yes	?	No	?	Yes
• Request to read from a paper, manuscript, or the like	?	?	No	No	M	Yes
• Request to withdraw a motion	?	?	No	No	M	Neg.
• Request to be excused from a duty	Yes	?	Yes	Yes	M	Neg.
• How nominations may be made	Yes	Yes	No	Yes	M	Yes
• Close nominations	Yes	Yes	No	Yes	⅔	No
• Reopen nominations	Yes	Yes	No	Yes	M	Neg.
• Close the polls	Yes	Yes	No	Yes	⅔	No
• Reopen the polls	Yes	Yes	No	Yes	M	Neg.
• Choose a method of voting	Yes	Yes	No	Yes	M	Yes
• Division of the assembly	No	No	No	No	—	—
• Create a blank	Yes	Yes	No	No	M	No
• Suspend the rules	Yes	Yes	No	No	⅔	No
• Object to the consideration of a question	No	No	No	No	⅔	Neg.
• Consider seriatim	Yes	Yes	No	Yes	M	No
• Point of no quorum	No	No	No	No	—	—
• Extend the time for the consideration of pending question	?	Yes	No	No	⅔	No
• Division of a question	?	?	No	Yes	M	No

[a]See 13.2–13.13 for explanation of question marks.

Point of Order

13.3 *Debatability.* Normally, the chair decides the question raised by the point of order. However, if the chair is in doubt and submits the question to the assembly, the point of order may become debatable because it is handled under the same rules as an appeal.

13.4 *Vote.* When a question (point) of order is placed before the assembly for decision, it requires a *majority* vote in the affirmative to carry the motion as opposed to only a *tie* vote needed to sustain the chair on an appeal. *Note:* The chair should put the question on a point of order so that the affirmative vote will be in favor of allowing the proceedings to continue as if the point had not been raised.

Appeal from the Decision of the Chair

13.5 *Debatability.* There are four times when this motion is undebatable:

- When it adheres to an undebatable motion.
- When it concerns a transgression of the rules of speaking.
- When it relates to indecorum.
- When it relates to the priority of business.

13.6 *Vote.* A tie vote sustains the chair.

Read from a Paper

13.7 *Recognition.* Assuming the member making the request has already obtained the floor, he is at liberty to make a formal motion that permission be granted if, in making the request, he fails to receive general consent. Another member may also make this motion.

13.8 *Second.* If the motion is made by the member requesting permission, it must be seconded. If moved by another member after the request is made, it does not require a second.

Withdraw a Motion

13.9 *Recognition.* The maker of a motion does not need the consent of anyone to withdraw the motion if the question has not been stated by the chair. If stated by the chair, the question belongs to the assembly and the maker can make a formal motion for withdrawal if, after making a request, the assembly does not grant general consent.

13.10 *Second.* If moved by the member making the request, the motion must be seconded. If moved by another member, after a request has been made by the maker of the original motion to withdraw the motion, no second is required, the reason being that two members are in favor of the assembly considering the motion to withdraw, the one making the motion and the other who made the request.

Request to Be Excused from a Duty

13.11 *Second.* If an objection is raised to a member's request to be excused from a duty, the member may then put it in the form of a motion. This motion requires a second. If moved by another member, it does not require a second.

Extend the Time for Consideration of the Pending Question

13.12 *Recognition.* This motion may interrupt a member who has the floor when orders of the day are called for or announced. It is in direct response to a Call for the Orders of the Day. The two-thirds affirmative vote, if obtained, will offset the two-thirds negative vote needed to keep from returning to the orders of the day.

Division of a Question

13.13 *Recognition.* If the subject matter is *not* related, there is no need for recognition nor a second, inasmuch as it is a demand which must be acted on by the chair. If the subject matter is related, it requires recognition and a second.

POINT OF ORDER (RNOR, p. 212)

13.14 The purpose of this motion is to enforce the rules or orders of the assembly. It invites the attention of the chair to a breach of procedural rules or the unethical conduct of a member.

Rules

13.15 The rules governing this motion are as follows:

- It is in order when another has the floor and may interrupt a speaker.
- It does not require recognition.
- It does not require a second.
- It is not debatable—see exception (paragraph 13.3)
- It is not amendable.
- The chair normally rules on the motion; majority vote if put to a vote.
- The vote, if taken, may not be reconsidered.

Form

13.16 "I rise to a point of order."
"Mr. President, I call the gentleman to order."
"Point of order!"

Precedence

13.17 This motion takes precedence over any pending

Table 13.2. Mnemonic Aids to the Classification of Incidental Motions

Debatable

Point of order—when the chair is in doubt and submits this motion to the assembly for decision
Appeal—except in the following instances:
- When it pertains to indecorum
- When it pertains to transgression of the rules of speaking
- When it pertains to the priority of business
- When the appeal adheres to an undebatable question.

Request to be excused from a duty

Amendable

How nominations may be made	Close the polls
Close nominations	Reopen the polls
Reopen nominations	Choose a method of voting
Division of a question	Request to be excused from a duty
Consider seriatim	

Require a Two-Thirds Vote for Adoption

Suspend the rules	Object to the consideration of a question (two-thirds negative to sustain)
Close nominations	
Close the polls	

Extend the time for the consideration of the pending question.

Reconsiderable

Appeal	Read from a paper
Choose a method of voting	How nominations may be made

Negative Vote Only May Be Reconsidered

Reopen nominations	Withdraw a motion
Reopen the polls	Object to the consideration of a question

Request to be excused from a duty

question out of which it may arise. It yields to all privileged motions, and if it adheres to the pending question(s), it yields to a motion to lay the main motion on the table.

13.18 If it does not adhere to the pending question(s) and the point of order is raised while *any* subsidiary motion is immediately pending, *no* subsidiary motion can be made until the point of order is disposed of, but any privileged motion can be moved and must be disposed of first.

Application

13.19 A point of order may be applied to any breach of the assembly's rules. No subsidiary motion may be applied to it as long as it is being ruled upon by the chair.

13.20 The subsidiary motions to limit or extend debate or to move the previous question may be applied if the chair submits the point of order to the assembly for decision, thus making it debatable.

Other Characteristics

13.21 The ruling of the chair on a point of order may be appealed. If referred to the assembly for a decision, the decision of the assembly, as expressed by its vote, cannot be appealed.

13.22 When placed before the assembly for a decision, a point of order is handled like an appeal, and like an appeal, it is debatable or undebatable under the same rules as those governing an appeal.

13.23 The chair, as in the case of an appeal, may speak twice—once at the beginning of the discussion and then again at the end. Other members of the assembly may speak only once.

13.24 It requires a majority vote when a point of order is put to a vote. This does not necessarily mean that the point of order is sustained. It depends on the wording of the question. In the case of a transgression of the rules of speaking, the chair should put the question so that an affirmative vote will permit the transgressor to continue as though the point of order had never been raised. "As many as are in favor of permitting the member to resume speaking say aye." However, in instances less clearly defined, the chair can put the question so that an affirmative vote will sustain the point of order. "Those who consider the point of order to be well taken say aye."

13.25 Important differences exist between the rules governing a point of order that has been placed before the assembly for a decision and an appeal from a ruling of the chair. These differences are:

- When a point of order is raised, it does not require a second, but an appeal from a ruling of the chair does.
- It requires a majority vote to sustain the question (not necessarily the point of order) when the point of order is put to a vote. A tie vote sustains the decision of the chair in an appeal.
- The vote taken on a point of order may not be reconsidered. The vote taken on an appeal may be reconsidered.

13.26 A point of order must be raised at the time the breach occurs, except that it is never too late to raise a point of order against violations of a continuing nature.

APPEAL (RONR, p. 218)

13.27 An appeal is an incidental motion to reverse a ruling of the chair.

Rules

13.28 The rules governing this motion are as follows:

- It is in order when another has the floor if it is made immediately after the chair's ruling.
- It does NOT require recognition.
- It requires a second.
- It is usually debatable.
- It is NOT amendable
- Majority vote decides the appeal, however, a tie vote sustains the chair.
- The vote may be reconsidered.

Form

13.29 "I appeal from the decision of the chair."

Precedence

13.30 An appeal takes precedence over any question pending at the time the chair makes a ruling from which the appeal is made. An appeal yields to all privileged motions that are in order according to the precedence of motions. It yields also to applicable incidental motions.

13.31 Under certain conditions a debatable appeal yields to the five highest subsidiary motions, provided they are in order according to the precedence of motions.

Application

13.32 An appeal can be applied to any ruling except: (a) when a point of order is raised while an appeal is pending; (b) when the appeal is dilatory; or (c) when the chair correctly rules on a matter that is obviously true.

When Debatable

13.33 If an appeal *adheres* to the pending question, only the motions to modify debate or the previous question can be applied to the appeal alone; however, the subsidiary motions can be applied to the main question, and if the question is committed, postponed, or laid on the table, the appeal goes with the main question.

13.34 If the appeal *does not adhere* to the pending question, it can have the five highest subsidiary motions applied to it.

When Not Debatable

13.35 If it *adheres* to the pending question, the appeal does not yield to any subsidiary motion except to lay on the table, when that motion is applied to the main question.

13.36 If it *does not adhere,* it yields to no subsidiary motion.

13.37 The motion is usually debatable but there are circumstances when it is not. These circumstances arise when (1) it relates to indecorum, (2) when it pertains to a transgression of the rules of speaking, (3) when the immediately pending question (to which it adheres) is not debatable, and (4) when it pertains to the priority of business.

Other Characteristics

13.38 In strongly contested situations, the chair may welcome an appeal for it relieves him of responsibility by placing it on the assembly itself.

13.39 The chair's answer to a parliamentary question

asked by a member of the assembly is merely an opinion and not an official act, therefore it cannot be appealed even if the answer is wrong. For example, in response to a parliamentary inquiry from a member of the assembly, the chair states that a certain motion is in order. This answer represents the chair's *opinion* and an *opinion* cannot be appealed. However, based on this opinion, the member who made the inquiry then makes the motion. If the motion is not in order, another member can raise a point of order, giving as his reason the fact that the motion is out of order. The chair would then have to *rule* on the point of order and such a *ruling* can be appealed.

13.40 The chair's announcement of a vote is not a ruling and is not subject to an appeal. A member, however, may call for a division of the assembly, more often simply called division, which is a demand, not to be ignored, that the vote be retaken. Such a call does not require recognition by the chair. It can be made at any time after the negative vote has been taken and is in order until the chair states the question on another motion. This call for a division (sometimes put in this form—"I doubt the vote.") requires the chair to immediately retake the vote as a rising vote, but not necessarily a counted vote, unless the chair, on his/her own initiative, chooses to count. A count can also be ordered by a majority vote of the assembly on a motion ordering the chair to count the vote.

13.41 The chair may speak twice to an appeal from his ruling—at the beginning of debate, to explain his reason, and at the end in rebuttal.

13.42 When an appeal is made from a ruling of the chair, the chair states clearly the exact question at issue and the reason for his decision, if he thinks such explanation necessary. Then he puts the question as follows: "Shall the decision of the chair be sustained?"

13.43 The vote is taken so that the affirmative vote will be in favor of sustaining the chair's ruling. A tie vote will sustain the chair. (This is an exception to the rule that a tie vote defeats a motion.) The chair may vote to create a tie.

SUSPEND THE RULES (RONR, p. 222)

13.44 An incidental motion is used when the assembly wishes to do something that cannot be done without violating its own rules but which does not conflict with the bylaws or fundamental rules of parliamentary law. Specifically, it can suspend special rules of order, rules of order, and standing rules.

Rules

13.45 The rules governing this motion are these:

- It is not in order when another has the floor.
- It requires recognition.
- It requires a second.
- It is not debatable.
- It is not amendable.
- It requires a two-thirds vote, except that a majority vote will suspend ordinary standing rules or the standing rules of a convention.
- The vote may not be reconsidered.

Form

13.46 "I move to suspend the rules and take up. . . ."

Precedence

13.47 A motion to suspend the rules takes precedence over the motion to which it applies when business is

Table 13.3. The Relationship of an Appeal to Subsidiary Motions

Debatable	Undebatable
Adheres to the pending question Rule 1. Only two subsidiary motions may be applied to the appeal alone: a. Limit (Extend) Debate b. Previous Question 2. All subsidiaries may be applied to the pending question and, if the motions to commit, postpone to a definite time, or lay on the table, are applied to the main motion, the appeal goes with it.	Adheres to the pending question Rule When an undebatable appeal adheres to the pending question(s), no subsidiary motion can be applied to it alone; but the main question can be laid on the table, and the appeal then goes to the table with the main question and all adhering motions.
Does NOT adhere to the pending question Rule The five highest subsidiaries may be applied to the appeal.	Does NOT adhere to the pending question Rule None of the subsidiary motions may be applied to the appeal. Undebatable When: • It relates to indecorum. • It relates to the transgression of the rules of speaking. • It relates to the priority of business. • It is applied to an undebatable motion.

pending. It can be made at any time even if no question is pending.

13.48 It yields to the motion to lay on the table, to all privileged motions and to incidental motions arising out of itself.

13.49 If it relates to the priority of business, it does not yield to a Call for the Orders of the Day.

Application

13.50 It can be applied to any rule of the assembly except the bylaws. No subsidiary motion can be directly applied to suspend the rules.

Other Characteristics

13.51 The adoption of the motion to suspend the rules permits nothing else to be done under the suspension except that which has been specified.

13.52 Among the rules that cannot be suspended are those contained in the bylaws (with the exception of clauses that provide for their own suspension) or those protecting the basic right of members. For example, a rule requiring previous notice protects the absentees.

13.53 In a motion to suspend the rules, the particular rule or rules to be suspended are not mentioned, but the specific purpose must be stated, for example:

I move to suspend the rules and permit the chairman of the membership committee to make his report at this time.

I move to suspend the rules and take up the motion relating to . . . , which was scheduled for consideration at 3:00 P.M.

13.54 When it is obvious that the adoption of a motion to suspend the rules will be followed by action on another motion, the two motions can be made simultaneously. This is an exception to the general rule that only one motion may be made at a time.

13.55 A motion to suspend the rules cannot be renewed for the same purpose at the same meeting unless unanimous consent is given. However, it can be renewed for the same purpose after adjournment of a meeting even if the next meeting is held on the same day.

13.56 When a motion to suspend the rules is not controversial, time may be saved by using unanimous consent: "I ask unanimous consent to permit our speaker to address the assembly at this time as his plane is due to leave before this meeting adjourns." The chair should then ask if anyone objects. If there is an objection, the chair proceeds to take the vote on suspending the rules, just as if a formal motion had been made.

13.57 An ordinary standing rule that does not relate to parliamentary procedure may be suspended by a majority vote.

13.58 Suspension of a convention standing rule (except one prescribing the parliamentary authority) can be suspended for a particular purpose by a majority vote even if the rule required a two-third vote for adoption. (See RONR, p. 518, footnote.)

13.59 A member moving to suspend the rules may give a brief reason for making this undebatable motion, so that the assembly can vote intelligently on the motion.

OBJECT TO THE CONSIDERATION OF A QUESTION (RONR, p. 227)

13.60 A motion objecting to the consideration of a question is an incidental motion whose purpose is to prevent an original main motion from being considered by the assembly.

Rules

13.61 The rules governing this motion are these:

It is in order when another has the floor.
It does *not* require recognition.
It does *not* require a second.
It is not debatable.
It is not amendable.
It requires a two-thirds *negative* vote to sustain the objection.
Only the *negative* vote may be reconsidered.

Form

13.62 "I object to the consideration of the question."

Precedence

13.63 This motion takes precedence over original main motions and petitions or communications that are not from a superior body.

13.64 It yields to (1) the motion to lay on the table (when this motion is applied to the main question to which it objects, (2) to all privileged motions, and (3) to incidental motions arising out of itself.

Application

13.65 It cannot be applied to an incidental main question. No subsidiary motion can be applied to it alone, but while it is pending, the main question can be laid on the table, and the objection goes to the table with the main question.

Other Characteristics

13.66 Objection to the consideration of a question can be raised only before there has been any debate or any subsidiary motion stated by the chair.

13.67 In some respects, object to the consideration of a question is similar to raising a point of order. The chair, on his own initiative, can submit his objection of this kind to a vote, just as he or she can raise a question of order.

13.68 There are important differences between object to the consideration of a question and a point of order. Objection to consideration should not be used if a main motion is outside the society's objects as defined in the bylaws. The main motion, if made under these circumstances, should be ruled out of order.

13.69 If the objection to consideration is sustained by the required two-thirds negative vote, the main motion is dismissed for that session and cannot be renewed during the same session except by unanimous consent or by reconsideration of the objection. If the objection is not sustained, consideration of the main question proceeds as if no objection had been made. Even if the objection is sustained, the same motion can be introduced at any succeeding session.

13.70 When the objection is put to a vote in its correct form, members are asked to vote for or against consideration of the question objected to, not for or against the objection. For example:

A member rises, even if another has been assigned the floor and, without waiting to be recognized, addresses the chair as follows: "Mr. Chairman, I object to the consideration of this question."

The chair then states, "The consideration of the question has been objected to. Shall the question be considered?

"As many as are in favor of considering the question, please rise. . . . Be seated. Those opposed, please rise. . . . Be seated."

If the vote reveals two-thirds or more in the negative, the chair will say: "There are two-thirds opposed and the question will not be considered."

If the objection is not sustained by a two-thirds negative vote, the chair will state, "There are less than two-thirds opposed, and the objection is not sustained. The question is on the resolution [or motion]."

13.71 Remember, in putting the objection to a vote, the chair must be careful not to say, "Shall the objection be sustained?" He or she should always say, *"Shall the question be considered?"*

CONSIDER BY PARAGRAPH OR SERIATIM (RONR, p. 233)

13.72 The motion to consider by paragraph (or seriatim) is an incidental motion whose purpose is to provide for the consideration of separate sections or paragraphs of a long motion (or resolution) so that each may be debated and amended without dividing the motion.

Rules

13.73 The rules governing this motion are as follows:

- It is not in order when another has the floor.
- It requires recognition.
- It requires a second.
- It is not debatable.
- It is amendable.
- It requires a majority vote.
- The vote cannot be reconsidered.

Form

13.74 "I move that the resolution be considered seriatim" (or "by paragraph").

Precedence

13.75 This motion takes precedence over the main motion and over the subsidiary motion to postpone indefinitely. If applied to an amendment, it also takes precedence over that amendment.

13.76 It yields to all subsidiary motions except postpone indefinitely, amend, and limit or extend the limits of debate. It yields to all privileged motions and applicable incidental motions.

Application

13.77 Consider seriatim can be applied to main motions and amendments of such length and structure that the method is appropriate. It may not be applied to the main motion while an amendment to the motion is pending.

13.78 No subsidiary motion except amend may be applied to consider seriatim alone. The previous question may be applied for the purpose of stopping amendments.

Other Characteristics

13.79 When consideration by paragraph (consider seriatim) is pending, the main question which engendered its proposal can be referred to a committee, postponed to a definite time, or laid on the table. As an unresolved question, consider seriatim will follow the main question through any process to which it may be subjected. If or when the main question is returned to the assembly, consider seriatim is resumed as if no interruption had occurred.

13.80 If consider seriatim is adopted, each paragraph or section is opened to debate and amendment. After all paragraphs have been considered, the entire series is opened to further debate and/or amendments. At this time additional parts may be struck out or parts inserted. A single vote is taken on the adoption of the entire series.

13.81 If there is a preamble to the resolution, it is treated in the same manner as the resolution itself. If the previous question is ordered before the preamble is considered, it does not apply to the preamble unless expressly so stated.

13.82 Motions to commit, postpone definitely, or lay on the table can only be applied to the entire series. If adopted, they affect the entire main question immediately. When the question is returned to the assembly, consideration by seriatim is resumed at the point where it was interrupted.

13.83 If the motion to postpone indefinitely is made during consideration by seriatim, it is stated by the chair but is not debated or voted on until seriatim consideration is completed and the entire series is declared open to debate and amendment.

13.84 To consider seriatim is a normal and advisable procedure for extensive changes in the bylaws or the adoption of an original or revised set.

13.85 The chair may, with general consent, use this method on his own initiative, or he may suggest that the formal motion be made by a member.

13.86 It is the duty of the secretary to make editorial changes, renumbering of paragraphs, and so on.

REQUESTS AND INQUIRIES (RONR, p. 243)

13.87 There are several types of requests and inquiries a member can make:

Parliamentary inquiry
Point of information
Leave to withdraw or modify a motion
Request to read papers
Request to be excused from a duty
Request for any other privilege

The first two types of inquiry are responded to by the chair or by a member at the direction of the chair. The other requests can be granted only by the assembly.

Precedence

13.88 These inquiries take precedence over any motion with whose purpose they are connected. They yield to all privileged motions and other incidental motions. A motion to be excused from a duty also yields to all subsidiary motions except postpone indefinitely.

Rules

13.89 These inquiries are in order when another has the floor if they require immediate attention.

13.90 Parliamentary inquiry and point of information do not require a second.

13.91 The others do not require a second except when moved formally by the maker of the request. A motion to grant the request of another member does not require a second, since two members already wish the question to come up—the maker of the request and the maker of the motion.

13.92 None of these inquiries are debatable except a request to be excused from duty.

13.93 None are amendable except a Request to be Excused from Duty.

13.94 No vote is taken on a parliamentary inquiry or a point of information. Other requests require a majority vote to be granted. (*Note:* Unanimous consent is required to grant a request to withdraw a motion to reconsider or to withdraw previous notice of a proposed motion requiring such notice.)

13.95 Parliamentary inquiry and point of information are not subject to reconsideration.

13.96 Votes on request permission to modify a motion, to read papers, or for any other privilege may be reconsidered.

13.97 Vote on permission to withdraw a motion or on a motion to be excused from a duty are two motions in which only the negative vote may be reconsidered.

14 Motions That Bring a Question Again before the Assembly

(RONR, p. 64)

14.1 According to RONR, these motions are characterized as a class of motions that "serve the function described by the name of the class." This means that they are not grouped together as a certain "class" but are closely allied in that the purpose they serve is a common one. They are as follows:

- Amend Something Previously Adopted
- Rescind
- Discharge a Committee
- Reconsider
- Take from the Table.

14.2 The motions to amend something previously adopted, rescind, and discharge a committee are incidental main motions. These motions take precedence over nothing and can only be moved when no business is pending. Take from the table and reconsider are both unclassified.

14.3 The objects of these motions are as follows:

- Take from the table proposes to resume consideration of a question that was placed on the table.
- Rescind proposes to strike out in its entirety a question that has already been adopted.
- Amend something previously adopted moves to modify only part of the question that has already been adopted or to substitute a different version.
- Discharge a committee proposes to take a matter that had been referred to a committee out of the hands of the committee so that it may be considered by the assembly or dropped from consideration.
- Reconsider provides an opportunity for a question to be returned to the assembly in the form it was in before being voted on originally.

14.4 Two of these motions apply to questions that were disposed of temporarily: take from the table, which is applied to motions that were laid on the table, and discharge a committee.

14.5 Three of these motions apply to questions that have already been adopted or rejected: reconsider the vote, rescind the motion adopted, and amend a previously adopted motion.

TAKE FROM THE TABLE (RONR, p. 252)

14.6 The motion to take from the table provides a means whereby an assembly may resume consideration of a motion, or a series of adhering motions, that had been laid on the table.

Rules

14.7 The rules governing this motion are:

- It is not in order when another has the floor.

- It requires recognition.
- It requires a second.
- It is not debatable.
- It is not amendable.
- It requires a majority vote.
- The vote may not be reconsidered.

Form

14.8 "I move to take from the table the motion concerning. . . ."

Precedence

14.9 To take from the table takes precedence over a main motion that has been moved but not yet stated by the chair. It does not take precedence over a question that is pending. It yields to privileged and incidental motions but not to subsidiary motions.

Application

14.10 This motion can be applied to any question or to a series of adhering motions that were previously laid on the table. No subsidiary motion can be applied to it.

Other Characteristics

14.11 To take from the table may be introduced when no program or rule interferes or when business of a class to which the subject belongs is in order.

14.12 The making of this motion may not interrupt a series of motions connected with taking up a single item of business. It cannot, for example, be introduced:

- After a rule has been suspended to permit a certain main motion to be introduced.

- After another question has been laid on the table for the express purpose of introducing a specified motion.
- After previous action has been rescinded so that a conflicting main motion may be made.
- After a main motion has been voted down so that a member may, as announced, offer a different motion.

14.13 In these cases, it would be out of order to move to take from the table a question which, having no bearing on the matters being considered, not only would serve no useful purpose but would interfere with and obstruct consideration of the series of motions needed to complete the item of business.

14.14 A question laid on the table may be taken from the table during the same session or at the next session if it comes within a three-month period.

14.15 A question not taken from the table within the time limits prescribed dies but may be reintroduced as a new question.

14.16 A question laid on the table is taken from the table in exactly the same order as when laid on the table, with the following exceptions:

- The previous question or the motion to modify debate remains in effect only if the question is taken from the table during the same session.
- If the time for a proposed postponement has passed, the subsidiary motion to postpone is ignored.

14.17 Members who have exhausted their right to speak may not again speak to the question on the same day. This right is restored if the question is taken from the table on another day.

14.18 If the motion to take from the table is moved and

voted down, it may be renewed only after some further business is transacted.

RESCIND (RONR, p. 256)

14.19 The motion to rescind is used to countermand a previous action—to strike out in its entirety something previously adopted.

Rules

14.20 The rules governing this motion are as follows:

- It is not in order when another has the floor. However, notice of intent to offer this motion at the next meeting may be given if it does not interrupt a speaker.
- It requires recognition.
- It requires a second.
- It is debatable.
- It is amendable.
- It requires a majority vote with notice, or a two-thirds vote or a majority of entire membership without notice.
- Only a negative vote may be reconsidered.

Form

14.21 "In accordance with notice given at the previous meeting, I move to rescind the resolution adopted at the (month) meeting, 'That. . .'."

"I move that the resolution relating to __________ adopted on (date) be rescinded."

Precedence

14.22 This motion takes precedence over no other motion. It yields to subsidiary, privileged, or applicable incidental motions.

Application

14.23 The motion to rescind can be applied to any motion that has been adopted and to the affirmative result of an appeal that is, a vote that sustained the chair's decision provided that nothing has been done that it is too late to undo. Subsidiary, privileged, and applicable incidental motions may be applied to the motion to rescind.

Other Characteristics

14.24 Rescind may have both primary and secondary amendments applied to it, as is the case of any main motion. However, if the amendment exceeds the scope of the previous notice given, a two-thirds vote, rather than a majority vote, is required.

14.25 To rescind (or amend) a standing rule of a convention requires a two-thirds vote or a majority vote of all the delegates who have registered. However, an individual rule that requires only a majority vote for adoption may be rescinded by a majority vote if notice was given at least on the preceding day.

14.26 The motion to rescind is not in order when the question can be reached by calling up a previously made motion to reconsider.

14.27 The motion to rescind cannot be applied to something that has been done that cannot be undone. However, the unexecuted part of an order may be rescinded.

14.28 Rescind may be moved by any member, regardless of how he voted on the original question.

14.29 There is no time limit on the making of this motion.

Rescind and Expunge from the Minutes

14.30 This motion expresses extreme disapproval and orders the previous action not only rescinded, but the record of such action struck from the minutes of the organization.

Rules

14.31 The rules governing this motion are essentially the same as those governing the motion to rescind. There are, however, certain important differences:

- It requires a vote of the *majority of the entire membership* to expunge that which has been rescinded.
- If the motion is adopted, the secretary, in the presence of the assembly, draws a line through the words to be expunged, writes across them the words "Rescinded and Ordered Expunged," followed by the date and his signature.
- Words must not be erased or cut out; however, if the minutes are published, they are omitted.

14.32 A more workable solution is to rescind the previous action, which requires a majority vote with notice or a ⅔ vote without notice, and then adopt a resolution condemning the action which has been rescinded which requires a majority vote. This eliminates the necessity of obtaining a majority vote of the entire membership.

AMEND SOMETHING PREVIOUSLY ADOPTED (RONR, p. 256)

14.33 As its name implies, this incidental main motion is to amend something previously adopted—to change only part of the text or to offer a substitute.

Rules

14.34 The motions to rescind or amend something previously adopted are two forms of one motion, governed by practically the same rules. The only difference is expressed in the purpose as just stated.

Form

14.35 "I move to amend the resolution relating to . . . which was adopted at the last regular meeting by. . . ."

"I move to amend the minutes of __(date)__ by striking out the name of (name to be struck) and inserting in place thereof (name to be inserted) as the individual who made the motion to. . . ."

"In accordance with notice previously given, I move the adoption of the following amendment to the bylaws. . . ." (It must be noted that an amendment to the bylaws requires a two-thirds vote even with previous notice.)

DISCHARGE A COMMITTEE (RONR, p. 261)

14.36 This motion removes a matter referred to a committee before the committee has made a final report.

Rules

14.37 The rules governing this motion are as follows:

- It is not in order when another has the floor.
- It requires recognition.
- It requires a second.
- It is debatable. The debate can go into the merits of the question in the hands of the committee.
- It is amendable
- It requires a two-thirds vote or a majority vote under conditions stated in 14.41 and 14.44.
- Only a negative vote may be reconsidered.

Form

14.38 For a standing committee: "I move that the ways and means committee be discharged from further consideration of the resolution relating to. . . ."

For a special committee: "I move that the committee to which was referred . . . be discharged."

Precedence

14.39 The motion to discharge a committee takes precedence over no other motion. It yields to subsidiary, privileged, and applicable incidental motions.

Application

14.40 The motion to discharge a committee may be applied to any main motion or other matter referred to a committee about which the committee has not yet made a final report. All subsidiary and applicable incidental motions may be applied to this motion.

Other Characteristics

14.41 This motion requires only a majority vote under any of the following conditions:

- If the committee has failed to report at a time specified by the assembly.
- If the assembly is considering a partial or interim report of the committee.
- If notice to discharge was given at the previous meeting or in the call of the meeting.

14.42 Previous notice may not interrupt a speaker but can be given after another has been assigned the floor; while another question is pending; or after adjournment has been voted on, providing the chair has not yet declared the assembly adjourned.

14.43 Certain circumstances may justify the motion to discharge even though the committee is not at fault. The assembly may want to act on the question or drop the matter from further consideration.

14.44 To instruct the committee to report at a reasonable, specified time requires only a majority vote if the time for reporting had not been previously approved. If the time had been previously approved, to change the time requires a two-thirds vote without previous notice. If previous notice had been given, it requires only a majority vote.

14.45 The motion to reconsider the vote referring the matter to a committee may be used if the committee has not yet begun its task.

14.46 If the motion to refer a matter to a committee was made as a main motion, the matter so referred dies upon discharge of the committee unless another main motion is made to bring it again before the assembly.

14.47 If the motion to refer was made as a subsidiary motion while a question was pending, the question automatically comes before the assembly upon discharge of the committee; therefore, no motion is needed.

14.48 If a standing committee is discharged from considering a certain matter, the committee continues to exist even though relieved of this responsibility. If it is a special committee, it automatically ceases to exist.

RECONSIDER (RONR, p. 265)

14.49 The motion to reconsider prevents hasty decisions and prevents undesirable motions previously adopted from being carried out before they can be reconsidered.

14.50 This motion has a distinctly American origin. The

U.S. House of Representatives adopted it as a rule in 1802 and made it a motion now described by *Robert's Rules of Order Newly Revised* as a motion that brings the question again before the assembly. The motion to reconsider now makes possible the immediate reconsideration of a vote on the same day.

Rules

14.51 The rules governing this motion are as follows:

- It is in order when another has the floor, except that it cannot interrupt a person speaking.
- It does not require recognition.
- It requires a second.
- It is debatable when the question to which it applies is debatable.
- It is not amendable.
- It requires a majority vote.
- It may not be reconsidered unless the question during reconsideration is materially changed. (If reconsideration passes, the question whose vote is being reconsidered is returned to the assembly in the same form it was before the vote was taken. Suppose the question had been, "To purchase a desk and chair for the secretary" and, during reconsideration, a motion was adopted to add after the word secretary, "and new furnishings for the clubhouse." This makes it a new question and the vote on this question may be reconsidered.)

Form

14.52 "I move to reconsider the vote on the motion concerning. . . ."

"I move to reconsider the vote on the amendment to strike out. . . ."

Precedence

14.53 This motion takes precedence over any other motion except the motion to reconsider and enter on the minutes." Even after the assembly has voted to adjourn, the motion is in order if the chair has not declared the meeting adjourned.

14.54 This motion yields to the motion to reconsider and enter on the minutes."

14.55 Its rank varies. It has high privilege for entry but not for reconsideration. It takes the rank of the motion to be reconsidered. For example, if it is moved to reconsider the vote on a main motion, it takes the rank of the main motion, that is, it can be acted on only when no other business is pending. If it is moved to reconsider the vote on a motion other than the main motion, such as the motion to refer or to postpone to a certain time, it takes the rank of the motion to which it applies. Reconsideration is not in order when a motion of higher rank is pending.

Application

14.56 The motion to reconsider may be applied to the vote on any motion except:

- The negative vote on a motion that may be renewed within a reasonable period of time.
- An affirmative vote on a motion whose provisions have been partly carried out, except a motion to limit or extend limits of debate.
- An affirmative vote in the nature of a contract when the parties to the contract have been notified.
- Any vote which has caused something to be done which cannot be undone.
- A vote on the motion to reconsider unless, during reconsideration, the question is materially changed.

14.57 The four highest subsidiary motions may be applied. Of course, if reconsider is in itself undebatable, the previous question and the motion which modifies debate would not apply. The three lowest subsidiaries cannot be applied to the motion to reconsider. It cannot be postponed indefinitely, amended, or referred to a committee.

Other Characteristics

14.58 The motion to reconsider can be made in an assembly only by a member who voted on the prevailing side. (This rule is modified in committee meetings. Refer to outline on "Boards and Committees.")

14.59 Any member of the assembly may second the motion. If a second withdraws the second, another member may second the motion to reconsider.

14.60 A member who did not vote on the prevailing side, or was absent, or did not vote when the vote was taken, cannot make the motion to reconsider the vote. (This rule is modified in committees.)

14.61 Any member can obtain the floor and call up the motion to reconsider a vote provided no other member has the floor. No second is necessary.

14.62 When the motion to which this motion is applied is debatable, it automatically gives one the right to debate the merits of the question it proposes to reconsider. However, if one has exhausted his right to debate the question proposed to be reconsidered (having already debated the question twice) and if reconsideration passes, he may not again debate the question on the same day.

14.63 If the previous question is ordered on the motion to reconsider, it affects also the motion to be reconsidered. If reconsideration passes, the question being reconsidered is also voted on without debate. This is an exception to the general rule that an unqualified motion for the previous question pertains only to the immediately pending question.

14.64 The motion to reconsider must be made on the day the vote was taken on the motion proposed to be reconsidered or on the next succeeding day. (Legal holidays and a day in recess do not count.)

14.65 When a motion to reconsider is laid on the table or postponed to a certain time, all adhering motions go with it. If tabled and not taken up before the end of the next business session for organizations which meet within a three month period or the end of the current session for those that do not meet as often as quarterly, the motion to reconsider automatically expires.

14.66 The motion to reconsider can prevent any action to be taken on the question whose vote is to be reconsidered until the end of the next business session, provided the next business session is within a three month period. This is considered the control period; however, it does not prevent the motion to reconsider being called up at any time during this period. It could, if in order, be stated by the chair immediately after being made. If reconsider is voted on and is lost, the question, whose vote it had proposed to reconsider, is immediately released from its control and the action that was suspended can be reinstituted. In organizations that do not meet as often as quarterly (within a three month period) the control of the motion to reconsider is exhausted at the end of the session at which it was made. As an example, in an organization holding an annual convention, the control period of the motion to reconsider would last until the last meeting on the last day of the convention.

14.67 As noted in the Rules Governing section under

each motion, there is one motion in which only the affirmative vote may be reconsidered; there are motions in which both the affirmative or negative vote may be reconsidered; and there are motions in which only the negative vote may be reconsidered.

14.68 Reconsideration may not be moved while in committee of the whole, but the vote on a motion to go into the committee of the whole may be reconsidered.

14.69 If subsidiary or incidental motions adhere to the main motion, reconsideration can be applied in such a way that the reconsideration takes place while the main motion to which the subsidiary or incidental motions adhere is pending, either before the main motion is voted on or when it is being reconsidered. For example, if the intent is to reconsider a secondary amendment while the main question is still pending, the primary amendment must also be reconsidered. If the main question has been voted on, the secondary amendment, primary amendment, and the main question must all be reconsidered. One motion to reconsider should be made covering the votes on these three motions.

14.70 Affirmative votes on amending bylaws cannot be reconsidered. Negative votes may be reconsidered.

RECONSIDER AND ENTER ON THE MINUTES (RONR, p. 281)

14.71 This motion to reconsider and enter on the minutes prevents a temporary majority from taking advantage of an unrepresentative attendance at a meeting to vote an action that is opposed by a majority of the membership of an organization.

14.72 Although a special form of the motion to reconsider, this motion outranks the motion to reconsider and can be made even after the vote is taken on reconsider, providing the results of such vote has not been announced by the chair.

14.73 If a motion to reconsider is voted on and loses, the vote proposed to be reconsidered cannot again be reconsidered, and any action held up comes into full force, effective as of the first time the vote was taken. For this reason, a member who voted on the prevailing side of an unrepresentative minority, operating under circumstances that enabled the group to be a temporary majority, may purposely move to reconsider the vote on the action taken then vote to help defeat reconsideration. There is one way in which this action can immediately be frustrated: Move to reconsider and enter on the minutes before the vote on reconsideration is announced by the chair.

Points of Similarity and Difference

14.74 The motion to reconsider and the motion to reconsider and enter are similar in the following respects:

- Both have the same general objective.
- Both have high privilege for entry.
- Neither yields to the three lowest subsidiary motions.
- Both yield to the four highest subsidiary motions.
- After being made, either holds over consideration until the next business day, provided the next business day is within a three month period.

14.75 The motions differ in these respects:

- Reconsider may be made on the day the vote on the motion to be reconsidered was taken or on the next calendar day. (Holidays and recesses are not counted.)
- Reconsider and enter must be made on the same day the vote was taken on the question proposed to be reconsidered.

- Reconsider can be taken up at the same meeting in which it was made.
- Reconsider and enter stops all action on the day it is made except that it can be made at a previous meeting during the last day then called up at the last meeting of an organization that does not meet at least quarterly.
- Reconsider can be applied to any motion which is specified under the rules as being reconsiderable.
- Reconsider and enter can be applied only to votes that dispose of the main motion.

3

Boards, Committees, Elections, Bylaws, and Conventions

15 Boards

(RONR, p. 399)

15.1 Boards and committees are important in assisting the assembly of an organization conduct the organization's business efficiently. This chapter treats the functions of boards, the next chapter the functions of committees. Figure 16.1 presents a schematic classification of both.

15.2 A board is appointed to act in a managerial and administrative capacity between meetings of the assembly. In different organizations, boards known as executive boards, boards of managers, boards of trustees, boards of directors, and so on.

15.3 The bylaws should specify who shall be members of the board, the powers delegated, how often the board should meet, its quorum and any other special rule or rules the organization feels is needed to control its operation.

15.4 An executive board usually consists of the officers of the organization and the chairmen of its standing committees. The bylaws may make provision, however, for others to participate in the executive board—for example, ex officio board members, who may or may not be members of the society. The governor of the State of Virginia is ex officio a member of the board of the Virginia Military Institute.

Powers and Limitations

15.5 A board has only such powers as are delegated to it by the organization's bylaws. As a general rule, the board cannot delegate its authority but may appoint subcommittees to work under its supervision. Such committees always report to the board.

15.6 A board enjoys powers seldom given to an ordinary committee, and these powers should not be abused. Great care must be taken that the board does not exceed the authority granted to it by its parent organization.

Conduct of Business

15.7 A board must meet with a quorum present in order to legally transact business. Even unanimous consent of members, outside of a meeting, cannot be considered a legal act of the board. Such general consent must be ratified at a legally called meeting.

15.8 Business is transacted in large boards under the same rules of procedure that govern deliberative assemblies: members address the chair, motions are seconded, debate is limited as in an assembly.

15.9 In small boards the procedure follows much the same pattern as large boards with the following exceptions:

- Motions need not be seconded.
- There is no limitation on the number of times a mem-

ber may speak, but the general rule that no one should be permitted to speak twice while one who has not spoken is seeking the floor should be followed.
- The motions to limit debate or the previous question are usually considered out of order.
- The chairman may take an active part in the discussions and even introduce motions without leaving the chair.
- Subjects may be discussed without the formality of a motion.
- Members need not rise to introduce motions or to debate.
- The chairman must take a vote on all questions unless the action taken is agreed to by general consent.
- All votes taken are formal, usually taken by voice or a show of hands.

Despite this informality, it behooves the chair to maintain control so that the purpose of the meeting is accomplished.

15.10 A quorum in a board is the majority of its membership unless otherwise specified in the bylaws of the parent organization.

15.11 Minutes of the board are not normally read at a meeting of the association. They may be ordered read by a majority vote if previous notice has been given or by a two-thirds vote or the vote of the majority of the membership without such notice. They are read, however, at the following meeting of the board for approval or (if needed) for correction before being filed.

Reports

15.12 The board makes an annual report to the parent organization and such other reports as the organization requires. These reports should always be in writing and signed only by the chairman of the board, who is usually the president of the organization, and the secretary.

15.13 Reports should be summarized so as to contain only matters of importance and actions taken by the board which will be of interest to the parent organization.

15.14 The secretary usually makes the report. However, any member may be authorized to make such a report and move the adoption of any resolution presented.

15.15 Every board should consider that an essential part of its duties is to present a resolution to carry into effect its recommendations. It should *never* leave this responsibility to others.

15.16 A society may adopt *in toto* a board's report or any part thereof. It may amend before adoption, but any change should be clearly marked so as not to obscure the original report.

Formation of Boards

15.17 Although the board itself has a continuing existence, any change in personnel, which usually occurs at the end of an administration and with the election of new officers, is tantamount to the election of a new board even though the change affects only a minority, perhaps one-third, of the board's membership.

15.18 Vacancies are filled by the appointing authority. Individual replacement of members does not bring into being a new board.

15.19 All unfinished business falls to the ground with the election of a new board.

16 Committees

(RONR, p. 406)

EXECUTIVE COMMITTEES

16.1 An executive committee may be classified as a board within a board. It is an independent entity that functions on its own responsibility between meetings of the board. An executive committee should not be instituted merely for the sake of form. A small organization that meets frequently usually does not need both an executive committee and a board within the structure of its organization. As a general rule, an executive board, which would include the members who would be on the executive committee, can more efficiently serve the purpose of such an organization.

16.2 The membership of the executive committee is usually specified in the organization's bylaws, rather than left to the choice of the full board.

16.3 Many organizations specify that the executive committee be composed of the officers of the organization. In keeping with this policy, these organizations also specify that the full board be composed of the officers and chairmen of standing committees.

16.4 The executive committee is usually given power to act as the board between meetings of the board. Although composed of some members of the board, it is not considered a subcommittee of the board. However, it cannot modify any action taken by the board.

16.5 The executive committee's quorum is a majority of its membership unless otherwise specified in the bylaws of the organization.

16.6 The executive committee should be required to make a report to the board of all action taken since the board's last meeting. Such a report is generally for information only and no action need be taken on the report.

ORDINARY COMMITTEES (RONR, p. 407)

16.7 An ordinary committee is a body of one or more persons, elected or appointed by an assembly, to consider, investigate, or take action on certain matters, or to do all these things.

16.8 Ordinary committees may be formed by an election with ballots, by nominations from the floor with viva voce election, by nominations from the chair with confirmation by voice vote, by appointment by the chair, or by a motion naming members of the committee.

16.9 The power to appoint a committee carries with it the right to appoint the chairman. If the chairman is not designated (when appointed by the chair, it is the first member named), the committee has the right to elect its own chairman.

16.10 The power to appoint also carries with it the right to fill any vacancy that may arise in the committee.

16.11 Ordinary committees are divided into two types: (1) standing committees, which have a continuing existence, and (2) special (ad hoc) committees, which go out of existence as soon as they have completed a specified task.

Standing Committees

16.12 A standing committee is a permanent committee of an organization placed in charge of a certain department or activity. Its members serve for a term corresponding to that of the officers of the organization and continue their duties until their successors are chosen.

16.13 The bylaws should list the name, composition, manner of selection, and duties of standing committees. In the event a standing committee is added to the number of standing committees, the bylaws should be amended to include the number so added.

16.14 This type of committee usually has standing authority to act for the society on matters of a certain class without instructions from the assembly. A motion to refer a question to a special committee on a matter which comes within the province of a standing committee so authorized is out of order.

16.15 The report of a standing committee should begin with the name of the committee and close, if applicable, with a resolution or resolutions. (See Fig. 16.3.)

Special Committees

16.16 A special committee is one created for a specific task. When its purpose is achieved and a final report made, it goes out of existence—for example, a nominating committee not listed in the bylaws as a standing committee.

16.17 When appointed to implement an order of the assembly, the committee should be small and consist only of those in favor of the action to be taken. When appointed for deliberation or investigation, the committee should be large enough so that all points of view of the organization are represented.

16.18 When given a specific task, a special committee should be told, in addition to its composition, what it is supposed to do and when it is expected to report.

16.19 When a committee is appointed "with power," it is authorized to take all steps necessary to carry out its assigned task.

16.20 The chairman or acting chairman should call a meeting of the committee as soon as possible after being assigned a duty. If the chairman or acting chairman is negligent in this respect, any two members may call a meeting of the committee.

16.21 The report of a special committee should begin with what the committee was instructed to do and close with a resolution, if recommendations for action is included in such report. (See Fig. 16.2.)

Conduct of Business

16.22 Committees conduct business in the same manner as in small boards. However, the motions to limit debate or the previous question are not allowed in a committee. A quorum is a majority of the membership of the committee unless otherwise stated in the bylaws of the organization.

16.23 The motion to reconsider a vote can be made regardless of the time that has elapsed since the vote was taken as long as the question is still within the control of the committee. Reconsideration can be moved by a committee member who did not vote on the losing side, who did not vote at all, or who was absent when the vote was taken. Unless those who voted on the prevailing side are present or have been notified that reconsideration would be moved, the motion to reconsider requires a two-thirds vote for adoption.

Reports

16.24 The chairman of the committee usually makes the committee's report to the assembly. Except for a brief verbal report to a small assembly, all reports should be written. Use the third person in writing reports—the report is a committee's report, not the chairman's.

16.25 A committee report can contain only what has been agreed to by a majority vote of the committee at a properly called meeting for which every member was notified and a quorum was present. If it is impractical to bring the committee's members together for a meeting, the report can contain what is agreed to by the majority of the committee only if its membership is comprised of individuals from different sections of the country and these individuals were appointed with the understanding that the committee's work would be done by correspondence. On the other hand, if the committee can reasonably be expected to meet and fails to do so, its report can contain only what has been agreed to by every member. (RONR, p. 418).

Minority Report—The minority report, if any, is more properly called the "views of the minority." Its formal presentation to the assembly is a privilege the assembly may accord, not a right to be exercised by those in the minority.

16.26 According to RONR, if a detailed report is in order, the following form, with topics arranged in logical sequence, fulfills this requirement:

- A description of the way the committee undertook its charge
- The facts uncovered or the information obtained

- Findings and conclusions derived from the facts
- Resolutions to implement recommendations (See RONR p. 420.)

16.27 If it is of considerable importance, the report should be signed by all members concurring. If the report is of minimal importance, the committee can authorize the chairman to sign the report alone, in which case he adds the title "chairman" after his name.

16.28 If the report contains only a statement of fact or opinion, with no recommendation, no action need be taken by the assembly. If the committee's report contains recommendations requiring action by the assembly, these recommendations should be brought together at the end of the report and stated in the form of a resolution.

16.29 Reports requiring action should *always* be implemented by a resolution, or resolutions, as stated above. The reporting member then moves the adoption of the resolution. Without this motion, there is nothing before the assembly for its consideration. Such a motion, because it is made on behalf of the committee, does not require a second.

COMMITTEE OF THE WHOLE AND ALTERNATE FORMS
(RONR, p. 442)

16.30 The committee of the whole is a strategem employed by an assembly to resolve itself into a committee so that it can take under consideration a certain subject and discuss it with most of the freedom of a committee.

16.31 A committee of the whole has two alternate forms: (1) quasi (as if in) committee of the whole, and (2) informal consideration.

16.32 Committee of the whole is suited to large assemblies and is frequently used by legislative bodies but seldom by ordinary deliberative assemblies.

16.33 Quasi committee of the whole is suited to medium-sized assemblies with a membership in the range of fifty to one hundred members.

16.34 Informal consideration is suited to small assemblies and is perhaps the form most frequently used by ordinary deliberative bodies.

Similarities and Differences

16.35 Although there are marked differences in the manner in which business is conducted in the committee of the whole and its two alternate forms, there are certain points of similarity worth noting:

- The committee of the whole and both its alternate forms are composed of the entire assembly.
- Under each of the three procedures, any member may speak in debate on the main question and its amendments for the same length of time as is allowed in the assembly's rules as often as he can get the floor. He cannot, however, violate the regular rules of debate by speaking another time to the same question while a member who has not spoken on the question is seeking the floor.
- All votes taken are formal.

16.36 The differences in the conduct of business between a committee of the whole and its alternate forms are as follows:

Releasing the chair:

- In a committee of the whole, the presiding officer releases the chair and appoints another member to act as chairman, usually the vice-president.

- In a quasi committee of the whole, the presiding officer does not release the chair; he remains in the chair and presides.
- In informal consideration, procedure is the same as in quasi committee of the whole, and the presiding officer does not release the chair.

Recording proceedings:

- In a committee of the whole, the secretary (sometimes replaced by another member) keeps only a temporary record of the business transacted. These notes are not recorded in the minutes of the assembly. The minutes reflect only the circumstance of referral to a committee of the whole, the committee's report, and the action taken by the assembly after such report has been received.
- In a quasi committee of the whole, the procedure is the same as that of the committee of the whole except that the secretary is not replaced.
- In informal consideration, the secretary records in the minutes of the assembly the proceedings of the committee in its transaction of business as though the matter was being considered under the rules of a formal assembly.

Motions that are in order:

- In a committee of the whole, the only motions in order are the motions to adopt, to amend, and to "rise and report". However, incidental motions such as raising a point of order, appealing from a decision of the chair, or pertinent requests and inquiries are allowed.
- In a quasi committee of the whole, any motion that would be in order in the assembly is also in order in a quasi committee of the whole; however, if any motion except an amendment is adopted, it puts an end to the proceedings. The motion to rise is not used; the pre-

siding officer simply ends the proceedings and reports to the assembly.

- In informal consideration, any motion except those applying to the main question and its amendments come under the regular rules of debate. The motions to limit or close debate are in order and subject to the rules governing their use. When the main question is disposed of, informal consideration ceases without motion or vote. If the motion is still pending, it is possible to end informal consideration by adopting the motion "that the question be considered formally."

After action reports:

- In a committee of the whole, an after-action report of the committee is entered in the minutes of the organization, but, as with any committee, the report is treated as recommendations that need to be finalized by action of the assembly under its regular rules. When the committee is ready to report, the presiding officer resumes his or her position in the chair; the committee's chairman then reports the action taken, if any. If amendments were proposed, the chair states and puts to vote all proposed amendments under one vote, unless a member asks for a separate vote on one or more of them.
- In a quasi committee of the whole, an after-action report is made to the assembly by the presiding officer, who had not released his or her post during consideration of the matter referred to the committee. This report is treated in the same manner as the report of the committee of the whole, that is, reports are considered recommendations that require action by the assembly, amendments are put to vote in gross, and so on.
- In informal consideration, no after-action report is needed. All actions taken have already been recorded in the assembly's minutes. When the question being

considered has been disposed of, the chair simply announces that informal consideration has ended and that the formalities of the regular rules will be observed.

Fig. 16.1. Classification of Boards and Committees

Boards and committees are brought together in condensed form so that one can see at a glance the distinguishing characteristics of each in the list which follows:

Boards

Boards are considered a type of deliberative assembly rather than a committee and, as such, exercise more power than is usually given to an ordinary committee. A board is subject to the limitations imposed by the organization's bylaws and should keep in mind that it cannot exceed such limitations.

Executive Committees

Executive committees are usually composed of the elected officers of an organization. An executive committee functions at the highest level of authority; however, it cannot change an action taken by the board of which its members are an integral part.

Ordinary Committees

Ordinary committees are groups of appointed or elected members of an assembly to whom motions, or matters that require more information or detailed consideration, are referred and who report before final action is taken by the assembly. There are two types of ordinary committees: standing committees and special (ad hoc) committees.

Standing Committees

Standing committees are the permanent committees of an organization. They are usually provided for in a separate article in the bylaws which delineates their composition, manner of selection, and duties.

Special (ad hoc) Committees

Special (ad hoc) committees are appointed as the need arises. A special committee is appointed for a specific purpose and ceases to exist when it has completed its assigned task and presented its report to the organization.

Committee of the Whole

A committee of the whole consists of the entire assembly. This device to go into the committee of the whole, when adopted, relaxes the regular rules of debate and gives the members the freedom to debate a question as often as they can get the floor, a procedure not unlike that of a committee. This strategem is suitable to large (over one hundred) or legislative assemblies. A committee of the whole has two alternate forms: quasi (as if in the) committee of the whole and informal consideration.

Quasi Committee of the Whole

Quasi committee of the whole is a substitute form of a committee of the whole and is suitable to medium size (50–100) assemblies. The underlying principle is the same as that of the committee of the whole but certain parliamentary steps, such as the chair relinquishing his position as presiding officer, are omitted.

Informal Consideration

Informal consideration, a second alternate form of a committee of the whole, is suitable to small deliberative assemblies. It completely eliminates the repetitious action of making a committee's report to the assembly, for all of its proceedings during informal consideration is officially recorded in the organization's minutes.

Fig. 16.2. Example of a Detailed Report of a Committee

Anytown Parliamentary Law Club
Anytown, Virginia

The special committee appointed to investigate the feasibility of expanding the range of activities of our Club by the organization of study groups in established associations, educational institutions, and clubs in the area submits the following report:

> The committee met twice monthly during the summer months (June–August). Each of its three members were given individual assignments. One met with the president and other members of the Anytown Council of PTAs. Another visited and spoke with the executive secretaries of the three country clubs in our area, and the third arranged an interview with the director of continuing education of our local community college.
>
> The president of the Anytown Council of PTAs has invited us to send representatives from our Club to the council's first meeting of the new school year, which will be held in the auditorium of Central High School at 7:30 P.M. on September 8.
>
> The visit to two country clubs was nonproductive. However, Mr. John W. Davis, the executive secretary of the Anytime Country Club, was enthusiastic about the idea of a study group. He said he believed many of the lady members would be interested in having a member of our Club explain the program in detail. He has posted a notice on the Country Club's bulletin board asking

members interested to list their names with the office secretary.

The director of continuing education said it was a splendid idea and that he would include parliamentary law in the list of subjects to be offered the next semester if our Club would furnish an instructor.

In view of the results obtained, the committee recommends adoption of the following resolutions:

Resolved, That the Club arrange to have a delegation from our Club meet with the Anytown Council of PTAs.

Resolved, That one of our registered members be sent to meet with the lady members of the Anytime Country Club, if there are enough members interested to form a group.

Resolved, That we furnish an instructor for a class in parliamentary law at the community college if such a class is formed.

Signed: John W. Radcliff
Chairman

On behalf of the committee, I move the adoption of the resolutions stated.

Fig. 16.3. Example of a Report of a Standing Committee

The Fine Arts Club
of
Any Town, U.S.A.

Report of the Membership Committee

The membership committee has received and considered the membership application of Mr. A. Peale and Miss Ima

Motion. Both applicants have been carefully investigated, and the evidence indicates both to be upright, civic-minded citizens of Any Town. The Committee believes they will make desirable additions to the membership of our Club.

The Membership Committee is severely handicapped by lack of sufficient funds needed to publicize the many worthwhile activities and accomplishments of our organization. The Committee feels that an expanded program of publicity will spark an increase in membership revenue, which will accrue from an increase in the number of new members. Their dues will more than make up for the extra expense involved. Of the $200 allocated to the Committee for the current fiscal year, only $62 is left after a lapse of six months. The Committee will need at least $50 more to meet the inflated cost of stationery, stamps, etc.

For the reasons cited, the Committee recommends the adoption of the following resolutions:

Resolved, That Mr. A. Peale and Miss Ima Motion be admitted to membership in our Club, and

Resolved, That the budget be amended by increasing the appropriation of the Membership Committee by $50—from $200 to $250—and that the Miscellaneous Fund be reduced from $600 to $550.

Signed: John Bridgeman
Chairman

By direction of the Committee, I move the adoption of the resolutions just stated.

Fig. 16.4. Examples of Committee Reports on Matters Referred

Main Motion Referred

Committee recommends the motion be adopted.

CHAIR: Is the committee to which was referred the motion "That we rent as a meeting place a room in the Carriage House of the First Baptist Church during the months of September through May inclusive" ready to report?

COMMITTEE CHAIRMAN: The committee to which was referred the motion "That we rent as a meeting place a room in the Carriage House during the months of September through May inclusive" recommends that the motion be adopted.

CHAIR: You have heard the committee's favorable report. The motion referred to the committee is "That we rent as a meeting place a room in the Carriage House of the First Baptist Church during the months of September through May inclusive." The question is on the adoption of the motion. Are you ready for the question?

Main Motion Referred

The committee recommends that the motion be not adopted.

CHAIR: Is the committee to which was referred the motion relating to the Carriage House ready to report?

COMMITTEE CHAIRMAN: The committee to which was referred the motion "That we rent as a meeting place a room in the Carriage House of the First Baptist Church during the months of September through May inclusive" recommends that, due to lack of parking space at the times of our regular meetings, the motion be not adopted.

CHAIR: You have heard the adverse report of the committee. The question is on the adoption of the motion "That we rent as a meeting place a room in the Carriage House of the First Baptist Church during the months of September through May inclusive," the recommendation of the committee to the contrary notwithstanding. Are you ready for the question?

Main Motion Referred

The committee recommends an amendment and moves its adoption.

CHAIR: Is the committee to which was referred the motion "That we rent as a meeting place a room in the Carriage House of the First Baptist Church during the months of September through May inclusive" ready to report?

COMMITTEE CHAIRMAN: The committee to which was referred the motion "That we rent as a meeting place a room in the Carriage House of the First Baptist Church during the months of September through May inclusive" recommends that the motion be amended by striking out the words "months of September through May inclusive" and inserting the words "next fiscal year beginning July 1," and that, thus amended, the motion be adopted.

By direction of the committee, I move the adoption of this recommendation. *(Hands to the chair the motion which was referred and, on a separate piece of paper, the amendment proposed.)*

CHAIR: You have heard the committee's report and its motion to amend the motion referred to it by striking out the words "months of September through May inclusive" and inserting in place thereof the words "next fiscal year beginning July 1." The question is on the adoption of the amendment. Are you ready for the question?

Main Motion Referred

The committee recommends a secondary amendment and moves its adoption.

CHAIR: Is the committee to which was referred the motion relating to the Carriage House ready to report?

COMMITTEE CHAIRMAN: The committee to which was referred the motion "That we rent as a meeting place a room in the Carriage House of the First Baptist Church during the months of September through May inclusive" with the pending amendment to add the words "At a cost not to exceed $15 a month" recommends that the amendment be amended by striking out $15 and inserting $20 and that, thus amended, the amendment and main motion be adopted.

On behalf of the committee, I move the adoption of these recommendations. *(Hands the motion referred with its pending amendment and, on a separate sheet, the proposed amendment to the pending amendment to the chair.)*

CHAIR:
You have heard the recommendation of the committee that the pending amendment be amended by striking out $15 and inserting $20 and that the motion "That we rent as a meeting place a room in the Carriage House of the First Baptist Church during the months of September through May inclusive," as thus amended, be adopted.

The question is on the amendment to the amendment to strike out $15 and insert $20. Are you ready for the question?

17 Voting

(RONR, p. 339)

17.1 A vote is the formal expression of the will of the assembly. The methods of voting are by voice, show of hands, rising, ballot, roll call, general consent, mail, and machine.

17.2 A *voice vote* is normally used to obtain a decision from the assembly by a majority vote.

17.3 A *show of hands* is used in a small assembly, and sometimes in committees, as a substitute for a rising vote.

17.4 A *rising vote* is used mainly to determine the result when a two-thirds vote of the assembly is required to obtain a decision; it is also used when a member calls for division of the assembly."

17.5 The *ballot vote* insures a measure of secrecy. It gives the individual member an opportunity to vote without disclosing the manner in which he voted. Sometimes this method is prescribed in the bylaws for the election of officers of the organization. If thus prescribed, any other means is null and void.

17.6 The taking of a *roll call vote* (yeas and nays) has the effect of placing on the record how each member votes. Therefore, it has exactly the opposite effect of a ballot vote.

17.7 *General consent* is used when the chair feels that the matter is of minimal importance and that valuable time may be saved by not having the formality of a vote. A single objection from a member will nullify the adoption of a motion by general consent.

17.8 *Mail* votes are usually resorted to when the membership of the organization is widely scattered. Any voting by mail must be authorized in the bylaws.

17.9 *Machine voting* is usually reserved for use by large organizations, mostly political in nature. It is also used by legislative bodies to expedite the process of recording the votes of individual representatives of a constitutionally established, public, law-making body. Careful preparation is needed to insure its proper use. (See RONR, p. 353.)

Majority Vote

17.10 A majority vote, without special qualifications, means more than half cast by persons legally entitled to vote, excluding blanks or abstentions, at a regular or properly called meeting at which a quorum is present.

Examples:

- 17 votes cast, majority is 9
- 18 votes cast, majority is 10
- 19 votes cast, majority is 10

Two-Thirds Vote

17.11 A two-thirds vote is at least two-thirds of the votes cast, excluding blanks and abstentions under the same conditions as stated under majority vote:

Examples:

- 45 votes cast, a two-thirds vote is 30
- 46 votes cast, a two-thirds vote is 31
- 47 votes cast, a two-thirds vote is 32
- 48 votes cast, a two-thirds vote is 32

A simple formula to use in calculating a two-thirds vote is to double the smaller number of votes. If, when doubled, the smaller number is equal to or less than the larger number, the result is a two-thirds vote. If the smaller number when doubled is greater than the larger number, a two-thirds vote has not been obtained. This procedure is especially helpful when used in large assemblies.

Plurality Vote

17.12 The largest number of votes cast for any candidate or proposition among three or more choices is a plurality. Unless authorized by a previously adopted special rule or unless stated in the bylaws, a plurality does not elect to office.

Preferential Vote

17.13 A special form in which less preferred choices of the voters is taken into account if no candidate or proposition attain a majority. (For specific details concerning the use of this vote, see RONR, pp. 357–60.)

Verifying a Vote

17.14 Any member, by calling for a division, can require a voice vote or a show of hands to be retaken as a rising vote, but it requires a majority vote by the assembly to order the chair to count the vote. If the chair announces that a two-thirds vote has been obtained and those on the losing side doubt the result, they are powerless to have it verified should those declared the winners choose to prevent a count.

18 Nominations and Elections

(RONR, p. 361)

NOMINATIONS

18.1 A nomination is a proposal that a person be elected to a specified position; in effect, it fills a blank in an assumed motion.

How Made

18.2 Nominations may be made by the chair, from the floor, by a committee, by ballot, by mail. The order in which these methods are listed corresponds to that in which they would be voted if all five were proposed in motions prescribing the method of nomination.

By the Chair

18.3 In organized societies, the chair may be asked to nominate committee members when the assembly wants to take advantage of the chair's knowledge and judgment yet still reserve the right to make the final decision. Under such circumstances, a member may move to strike out the name of one of the nominees but cannot move to strike out and insert another name because this would, in effect, usurp the chair's prerogative. It is up to the chair to suggest another name if the member's motion to strike out is adopted.

From the Floor

18.4 Floor nominations are usually taken immediately after receiving the report of a nominating committee as a prelude to the election of officers or members of a board or a committee. When nominations are called for by the chair, members need not rise except in a large assembly. No second is required.

18.5 A person may be nominated for more than one office even though the voting is on a single ballot. For example, he or she may be nominated from the floor for one office and nominated by a committee for another. If present, the nominee can select the office in which he or she wishes to serve. If absent, the assembly decides by vote the office to be assigned and then proceeds to elect another to fill the vacancy.

18.6 If any member objects, no one can nominate more than one person for a given office, until every member wishing to nominate another member has had an opportunity to do so.

By a Committee

18.7 Members of the committee should be elected far enough in advance to give them an opportunity to intelligently select a nominee for each office to be filled.

18.8 The committee should be *elected* either by the organization or, if the bylaws so provide, by the executive board. The chair should not be a member of this committee, even in an ex-officio capacity.

18.9 The presentation of the committee's nominating report proceeds as follows:

- When the chair calls for the report, the chairman or reporting member rises and reads the report in full.
- The report is *received* by the chair, but no motion is made to adopt.
- The report, when submitted to the presiding officer, should be signed by members of the committee. The chairman's signature is first, but the title of "chairman" is not used.
- The presiding officer rereads the report and then calls for nominations from the floor, beginning with the first vacancy listed. This call for nominations from the floor is required. (See RONR, p. 365.)

PRESIDING OFFICER: The next business in order is the report of the Nominating Committee.

CHAIRMAN, NOMINATING COMMITTEE: The Nominating Committee of the Centerville Council of PTAs submits the following nominations of officers for the coming year:

For president .... Mr. Jack Nixon
For vice-president .... Mrs. Iona Heart
For secretary .... Mrs. May Scribble
For treasurer .... Mr. Bud Jetnow

(Signed) *Jimmy Roosevelt*
Franklin Carter
Richard Kennedy

THE CHAIR: The nominating committee has made the following nominations of officers for the coming year:

For president .... Mr. Jack Nixon
For vice-president .... Mrs. Iona Heart

For secretary . . . . Mrs. May Scribble
For treasurer . . . . Mr. Bud Jetnow

Mr. Jack Nixon has been nominated for president. Are there further nominations for the office of president? *(It is in order for the chair to repeat the name of each member nominated by the committee before asking if there are any further nominations for that office.)*

18.10 After giving members of the assembly the opportunity to nominate members of their choice for each office, the chair may close nominations by general consent: "As long as there are no further nominees, nominations are declared closed." The same result can be obtained if a member moves to close nominations and the motion is properly seconded. This requires a two-thirds vote for adoption.

Nominations by Ballot

18.11 The purpose here is to indicate the preference of all members without electing. It is conducted in the same fashion as an electing ballot except that everyone receiving a vote is nominated. Members do not have the right to make additional nominations from the floor unless given that right by a majority vote of the assembly.

18.12 A motion to declare the nominating ballot the electing ballot destroys the advantages of a nominating ballot and, in effect, is the same as having an electing ballot without any nominations.

Nominations by Mail

18.13 Nominating by mail is useful in organizations with a scattered membership. A vote by mail must be authorized in the bylaws. It is generally reserved for use in important issues, such as an amendment to the bylaws or, in some instances, the election of officers. Steps should be taken to insure that all votes are cast by qualified voters. If the vote is to be secret ballot, certain procedures are in order. (See RONR, p. 356).

General Information

18.14 Nominations must conform to the procedures prescribed in the organization's bylaws.

18.15 Only those with voting rights can nominate someone for office.

18.16 A member has the right to nominate himself (herself) for an office. There is a difference between being a *candidate* and a *nominee.* One becomes a candidate simply by declaration of intent to seek the office. To become a nominee, however, requires the positive action of placing the name in nomination in accordance with the established rules of the organization.

18.17 Nominating committees have the right to nominate members of their committees, but this right should not be abused.

18.18 A member not nominated may be elected unless this is contrary to the bylaws.

18.19 The nominating committee may be either a standing committee or a special committee. If a standing committee, it should be listed as such in the bylaws. The fact that the bylaws contain a special provision prescribing the manner of selection of a nominating committee, delineating its duties and method of procedure, has no bearing on the case. It is *not* a standing committee unless listed as such in the article containing a list of standing committees.

18.20 Nominees do not leave the assembly room during an election. If prudent, they should vote for themselves.

18.21 A premature motion to close nominations should be ignored by the chair. The chair's response should be, "Are there any further nominations?"

ELECTIONS

18.22 When nominations have been completed, the assembly proceeds to the election. Voting is usually by ballot if there is more than one nominee for any given office. The bylaws may require the election to be by ballot and at the same time provide an exception when there is only one nominee for an office. If the bylaws are silent, then any of the usual methods of voting may be adopted by the assembly.

18.23 The bylaws should be understood and rigidly adhered to during elections as in all other cases. It is good procedure to have the parliamentarian, or some other member, read the section in the bylaws pertaining to elections immediately before an actual election takes place.

18.24 If the chair is a candidate for election, he is not obliged to surrender the chair unless the bylaws say he must.

18.25 A member holding two positions in the assembly such as secretary and treasurer (each of which has a vote) will nevertheless cast only one vote unless otherwise specified in the bylaws.

18.26 If the bylaws require a vote on a question to be by ballot, it must be done in that manner. Bylaws cannot be ignored, suspended, or violated even by unanimous vote. RONR says over and over again that *if the bylaws require an election to be by ballot, any other method is null and void,* and there is no election.

18.27 If there is no conclusive election on the first ballot, members who arrive late may vote on the second ballot.

18.28 "Number of votes cast" means the total number of votes cast for each individual office without regard to the number cast for any other office.

18.29 Custom has the force of law in voting procedures, as in other areas, until it is ordered stopped by action of the assembly. A motion to discontinue an established custom (to rescind) requires a two-thirds vote without notice or a majority vote with notice.

18.30 If bylaws contain no special provision for holding an election to fill a vacancy, such election may be held at any regular meeting with due prior notice to members.

18.31 To facilitate a recount if necessary, ballots are kept by the secretary for a reasonable period before being destroyed.

18.32 The presence of nonmembers who do not vote does not invalidate the results of an election.

Duties of Tellers

18.33 Tellers appointed by the chair are responsible for the distribution, collection, and counting of ballots.

18.34 Tellers can vote in elections. The fact that they have been assigned a specific duty does not deprive them of their rights as members.

18.35 In recording the votes from the ballots cast, the tellers ignore blank ballots and do not credit illegal ballots to any candidate. However, illegal ballots are taken into account in determining the number of votes cast for the purpose of computing the majority, providing the ballots were cast by those legally entitled to vote.

18.36 When two or more filled out ballots are folded

together, they are recorded as one illegal vote. If a blank ballot is folded with another ballot properly filled out, the blank is ignored, but the other is counted as a legal vote.

18.37 Although unintelligible ballots are counted as illegal votes, the mere misspelling of a name does not, by itself, invalidate the vote as long as the meaning is clear.

18.38 Counting the ballots is an important assignment. The chairman of the tellers should exercise great care to see that no one interferes with the tellers while they are engaged in this task.

18.39 If a member leaves one or more choices blank on a ballot containing more than one office to be filled, the blank spaces should in no way affect the validity of the spaces he has filled, and for each such space, he should be given credit for a legal vote. If, however, he votes for too many candidates for a given office, that particular section is illegal because it is impossible for the tellers to tell for whom the member desired to vote.

18.40 If the tellers are in doubt as to the legality of a vote and that vote affects the result, the tellers should bring the matter to the attention of the chair who in turn should immediately submit it to the assembly for a decision.

Tellers' Report

18.41 When the tellers return to the assembly hall, the chair says, "Are the tellers ready to report?"

18.42 The chairman of the tellers replies, "Mr. (or Madam) President, your tellers, having counted the ballots, submit the following report:

For President

Number of votes cast 96

Necessary for election 49
Mr. A received 54
Mr. B received 41
Illegal vote 1
Mrs. H. L. Johnson, ineligible.

"Mrs. Johnson has served two terms as president and under the provisions of Section 1, Article IV of the bylaws, is ineligible for reelection."

18.43 The report for other offices is made in the same manner. The number of votes cast in each instance is not necessarily the same. The majority necessary for election must be determined in each case according to the number of votes cast.

18.44 Having read the report, the chairman of the tellers hands the report to the chair who again reads the report announcing after the reading of each office the successful candidate (if any) who has been elected. Remember, it is the chair and not the chairman of the tellers who announces the election of the successful candidates.

18.45 For offices for which no candidate has attained a majority, the chair announces "No election" and continues reading until the tellers' report for all offices has been read. The chair then directs that new ballots be distributed and another vote taken for offices yet to be filled.

18.46 When repeated balloting for an office is necessary, the names of all nominees for that office are kept on the ballot unless the bylaws prescribe otherwise. It is possible that the nominee receiving the lowest number of votes can become the compromise candidate and be elected to office.

19 Contents of Bylaws

(RONR, p. 474)

Article I: Name

19.1 In unincorporated societies the full, exact, and properly punctuated name of the society should be given. In incorporated societies, or those with a separate constitution, this article may be omitted.

Article II: Object

19.2 The object of the organization should be concisely expressed, in a single sentence if possible.

Article III: Membership

19.3 This article usually consists of several sections. Classes of members should be listed, such as active members, associate members, affiliate members, student members, and honorary members.

19.4 Qualifications or eligibility for membership should be specified and include application and acceptance procedures, and the method of reviewing and voting on applications.

19.5 Required fees and dues should be specified in this article, unless this information is put in a separate article. This section may also include the date dues are payable (annually, quarterly, and so on), any delinquency grace period and procedure for notifying delinquent members, and the date on which members will be dropped for nonpayment of dues.

19.6 Other rules regarding membership that may be specified in the bylaws are these:

- Conditions under which resignations are acceptable.
- Reinstatement procedures.
- Voting rights may be suspended *only* if bylaws so state.
- Members may be assessed beyond payment of dues *only* if the bylaws authorize such action.
- Attendance at meetings may be required *only* if the bylaws contain special provisions for this.

Article IV: Officers

19.7 The bylaws should list all officers, including honorary ones, and show how they should be elected or appointed. Officers rank in the order listed. Directors are usually classified as officers.

19.8 Under the section devoted to duties of officers, a statement that "officers shall perform the duties prescribed by these bylaws and the adopted parliamentary authority" is usually sufficient.

19.9 If duties are numerous or extraordinary, an extra article or special section may be added. This has the advantage of collecting information in one place; however, care should be taken for failure to specify a certain duty may imply that it is not required.

19.10 The nomination and election of officers are often made the subject of a separate article. Regardless of whether it is made a separate article, the following information should be given:

- The method of nomination should be shown. If by a committee, the time and method of selection of the members of the committee should be stated, including their duties, the time of report, and so on.
- If nomination is limited to one candidate for each office, this should also be stated in the bylaws.

19.11 Ballot vote is usually prescribed for the election of officers. Provisions may be made for dispensing with the ballot vote when there is only one candidate for an office.

19.12 If election is to be by mail vote, by plurality vote, or by preferential voting, this must be expressly stated, and the details of procedure prescribed.

19.13 The length of the term of office should be prescribed. A fixed term is not recommended because, at the end of the time, there would be no officers if for some reason new ones had not been elected. (For the use of the term "or" in preference to the term "and" in stating the term of office, refer to RONR, p. 555.)

19.14 The method and the name of the body responsible for filling vacancies should be prescribed. Unless otherwise provided, notice must always be given to the body responsible for filling a vacancy.

19.15 The vacancy created by the loss of the president is filled by the vice-president. If a different method is desired, the bylaws must contain a specific provision outlining the manner in which the vacancy is to be filled.

19.16 The electing body automatically has the power to fill any vacancy other than that of the president unless otherwise provided by the bylaws. In some organizations, this responsibility is delegated to the executive board or the executive committee.

Article V: Meetings

19.17 Specify the day or days of a regular meeting, using such forms as ". . . the first and third Wednesday of each month."

19.18 If a provision is included that "unless ordered by the society (or "Executive Board"), the date may be changed for a single meeting or a particular occasion but not for several meetings. (See RONR, p. 483.)

19.19 Stringency can be avoided by establishing the hour of meeting under a standing rule. This duty may also be delegated to the executive board or executive committee.

19.20 Many organizations designate and set aside one of their regular meetings as the annual meeting. Such a meeting should include in its agenda provisions for the election of officers and the annual reports of boards, officers, and standing committees.

19.21 The bylaws should specify by whom special meetings may be called and the number of days notice required. Only business as specified in the call of the meeting may be transacted, unless the bylaws provide otherwise.

19.22 A quorum for all meetings should be established in a section of this article. In stating the requirement for a quorum, a positive integer (definite number) is preferred even though this number may have been calculated on the basis of a percentage of the membership. (This eliminates any confusion that could be caused by an abrupt change in total membership.) If the bylaws fail to specify the quorum, the quorum then becomes a majority of the total membership.

Article VI: Executive Board

19.23 An *executive board* usually includes officers; directors, managers, or trustees; and standing committees chairmen.

19.24 The bylaws should delineate the board's powers and set forth any special rules by which it is to conduct business. The bylaws should also state when and how often the board is to meet, its quorum, and so on.

19.25 The *executive committee* may be considered a board within a board. Although a subdivision of the board, it is not a genuine subcommittee. It functions between meetings of the board and, for the most part, acts independently on matters brought to its attention. It may not, however, modify any action taken by the board. It reports to the board any action taken. This report is for information only, and no action need be taken on the report.

Article VII: Committees

19.26 The bylaws should provide for the establishment of *standing committees,* which are usually few in number. Some of the most commonly used standing committees are bylaws, education, membership, program, budget-finance, and public relations. Additional standing committees may be authorized only if the bylaws contain such a provision.

19.27 The bylaws should list the name, composition, manner of selection, and duties of standing committees.

No other standing committees may be added unless the bylaws specifically authorize the president to appoint such standing committees as the society or executive board shall from time to time deem necessary to carry on the work of the society. If such authority is granted, and is implemented, the next publication of the bylaws should reflect such change or changes in its list of standing committees.

19.28 A standing committee usually has standing authority to act for the organization on matters of a certain class without specific instruction from the assembly. A motion to refer a question to a special committee on a matter that comes within the province of a standing committee is out of order.

19.29 The provision for appointment of *special committees* should be given in a section separate from that of standing committees.

19.30 Unless authorized by the bylaws, the president's authority is limited, and he may not appoint special committees other than those prescribed by the society, or the board if the bylaws so empower the board.

19.31 This section may provide also for the president to be ex officio a member of all committees except the nominating committee. Lacking this provision, the president has no vote in the committees, nor can he attend any of their meetings except by invitation.

Article VIII: Parliamentary Authority

19.32 The parliamentary authority should be prescribed in one sentence, such as:

Rules contained in the current edition of *Robert's Rules of Order Newly Revised* shall govern the Society in all cases to which they are applicable and in which they are not inconsistent with these bylaws and any special rules of order the Society may adopt.

Article IX: Amendment of Bylaws

19.33 The bylaws should always prescribe the procedure for their amendment, requiring at least advance notice given in a specified manner and a vote of at least two-thirds for adoption.

19.34 If the bylaws contain no provision for amendment, they may be amended at any business meeting (including a special meeting if notice is included in the call) by a two-thirds vote with previous notice or by a vote of the majority of the entire membership without such notice.

19.35 Amendments to the proposed bylaw amendment must be within the scope of the notice. For example, a proposed amendment to raise dues by five dollars as given in previous notice cannot be amended to raise dues in excess of such notice, say by six dollars.

19.36 Giving notice should be limited to *the* previous meeting rather than *a* previous meeting. Members are thus alerted and know the exact meeting in which the amendment will be voted on.

19.37 The manner of giving notice should be prescribed to fit the needs of the organization. For some, oral notice is sufficient; others may require written notice.

19.38 Amendments take effect immediately on adoption unless the motion to adopt contains a proviso specifying a different time—for example, by adding "with a proviso that. . . ." or "provided that this amendment will not go into effect until. . . ."

19.39 The wording of this article should avoid redundant phraseology such as "amend, alter, add to, or repeal," or "amend, alter, or in any way change." The word *amend* covers all.

Article for Nonprofit Organizations

19.40 The Internal Revenue Service has directed (Section 501 [c] [3]) that all nonprofit organizations include in their bylaws a statement as to the disposition of its assets in the event of dissolution. This normally would be contained in an article preceding the article on parliamentary authority.

19.41 A suggested wording of the article is as follows:

In the event of the dissolution of this organization, the assets remaining after payment of all costs and expenses of such dissolution shall be transferred or conveyed to one or more domestic societies engaged in charitable, religious, educational, or similar activities, provided however that said organization shall qualify under Section 501 (c) (3) of the Internal Revenue Code, and none of the funds or assets shall inure to the benefit of, or be distributed to, the individual members.

Other Special Articles

19.42 In addition to the basic articles, some organizations find it expedient to highlight other requirements by putting them into separate articles. Some of the most common are as follows:

- *Delegates* to the convention of a parent organization.
- *Dissolution clause* for nonprofit organizations.
- *Dues* are sometimes placed in a separate article after the one pertaining to membership.

Items 1 and 2 above are usually placed *before* the articles dealing with parliamentary authority and amendments.

20 Conventions

(RONR, p. 499)

20.1 The term *convention* refers to an assembly of delegates. Conventions vary in size, duration and complexity of operation: a small society may hold a one-day session consisting of two or three meetings in which all delegates are present; a large society may meet for several days with several sections meeting at the same time and then, in addition, hold one or two scheduled meetings for the entire body.

Bylaws

20.2 Bylaws are most important insofar as they concern the conduct of a convention in a regional, state, or national society. RONR states bylaws should:

- Authorize a periodic convention.
- Define its powers and duties.
- Fix its quorum.
- Specify its voting members.
- Describe the qualifications of its delegates, alternates, and the basis for determining their number.

- Describe the method to be used in electing delegates, alternates, and other voting members. (See RONR, p. 500.)

20.3 Bylaws should prescribe the conditions under which the constituent unit will be considered in good standing for the purposes of the right to representation. (This is usually the minimum number of membership.)

20.4 Representation usually depends on the size of the constituent unit. For example, the bylaws may state:

Each unit shall be represented by its president plus one additional delegate if the unit has more than a certain number; two additional, if the unit has twice that number or a major portion thereof.

20.5 To avoid a change of officers during the convention, bylaws should provide that the elected officers will take up their duties at the end of the convention or at some given future time.

Voting, Delegates, Caucuses

20.6 Voting membership is usually established:

- Through being an incumbent elected or appointed officer of the body on the level at which the convention is held.
- Through being an accredited delegate elected by the constituent body.
- Through a provision in the bylaws—"President of each club shall be one of the delegates."
- Or through an accredited elected alternate.

20.7 It is better to have each alternate ready to fill any vacancy than to have alternates "paired" with a particular delegate. The latter system is disadvantageous if both delegate and alternate of the same pair cannot attend.

20.8 Each unit should have as complete a representation as possible at the convention. This makes for a uniform standard of representation.

20.9 The temporary absence of a delegate does not entitle the alternate to make motions, speak in debate, or cast votes. An alternate must report to the credentials committee to be properly certified as having replaced the delegate before he or she can be considered eligible to participate.

20.10 Caucuses may be held prior to or during the convention.

20.11 The unit rule allows a delegation to cast its *entire* vote as the majority of its delegates decides, regardless of any other preference the minority may have.

Important Committees

20.12 The five most important committees are the credentials committee, the committee on standing rules, the program committee, the convention arrangements committee, and the resolutions committee.

Credentials Committee

20.13 The specific duties of a credentials committee are varied and spread over a considerable period of time. Among the committee's duties are the following:

20.14 Notify constituent bodies of the authorized number of delegates and alternates, eligibility requirements, and so on. This is usually included in the official "Call to Convention."

20.15 Check the list of delegates and alternates proposed by constituent units to see if they are eligible and within the limitation as to number.

20.16 Make suitable arrangements for the registration of delegates when they arrive at the convention.

20.17 Record each delegate as officially registered upon presentation of credentials and payment of registration fee.

20.18 Issue badge, (ribbon) the official program, and any additional relevant information.

20.19 Prepare the committee's first report to the convention, announcing the hour on which the report is based.

20.20 Record changes in the registration rolls.

20.21 Make at least two duplicate copies of the register—one to be submitted as an attachment to the Committee's report, and one for later use by the election tellers.

20.22 Contested seats, if any, should be omitted from the list, and the fact reported to the convention. This is seldom necessary in ordinary deliberative assemblies.

20.23 Chairman states, after completing report: "On behalf of the Committee, I move that the roll of delegates, hereby submitted, be the official roll of the voting members of the convention."

Committee on Standing Rules

20.24 The committee on standing rules is responsible for drafting rules for the operational procedures required for that particular convention.

20.25 These rules must in no way conflict with the bylaws, but they can involve modification of rules contained in the parliamentary authority prescribed in the bylaws.

20.26 A copy of the proposed standing rules should be handed to each delegate when he or she registers.

20.27 The report of the committee on standing rules is presented to the convention immediately after the adoption of the report of the credentials committee.

20.28 The parliamentarian should be consulted on the standing rules. He often prepares the first draft.

20.29 Reading the rules before moving their adoption may be omitted if every delegate has a copy and the rules generally do not change from year to year—provided also that a firmly established custom of the organization permits this reading to be omitted.

20.30 The rules generally require a two-thirds vote for adoption inasmuch as they nearly always include provisions which can be imposed only by a two-thirds vote.

20.31 To amend or rescind the standing rules of a convention requires a two-thirds vote or the vote of a majority of all the delegates or other "voting members" of the convention who have been registered. An exception to this is that a rule individually adopted by a majority vote may be amended or rescinded by a majority vote. (Notice should be given at least the previous day for a majority vote to be effective.)

20.32 Any standing rule of a convention may be suspended for a particular purpose by a majority vote. (Such suspension brings the applicable rule of the parliamentary authority into force, as if the standing rule had not been adopted.) This is true even if the standing rule initially required a two-thirds vote. (See RONR, p. 518n.)

Program Committee

20.33 A program committee plans and submits a proposed schedule of meetings, proceedings, and special events of the convention. This is extremely important. A convention must be able to transact a large amount of business in as short a time as possible.

20.34 Many details need to be decided prior to the convention. The program is more complex than for a committee of the same type in a local unit.

20.35 The following is a general outline of the duties of the program committee:

- Act in cooperation with the arrangements committee to engage outside speakers & entertainers.
- Notify each voting member of the time a particular matter will come before the convention.
- Timing is an especially important factor in arranging the schedule or agenda, and strict adherence is necessary so that the convention can complete its work as prearranged.

20.36 The program may be divided into two parts: the first part lists the times and places for special events and the hours for the call to order, adjournment, and scheduled recess of business meetings; a second part lists the items or classes of business set for each meeting.

20.37 Adoption is normally moved by the reporting member if he is a voting member. If not, it could be moved by the recording secretary or a voting member. If the voting member is not a member of the committee, a second is required.

20.38 If changes are necessary, and they often are, the chairman makes his report by saying, "The Program Committee recommends the following modifications in the program now in the hands of each registrant." Clearly state each change, with reference to page and line in the program. "By direction of the Committee, I move that, with these changes, the program be adopted."

20.39 To change the program after adoption requires a two-thirds vote, or the vote of the majority of all the delegates or other "voting members" of the convention who have been registered, or unanimous consent, which can usually be obtained without difficulty if departure from the program is justified. (See RONR, p. 526.)

20.40 Normally, the minutes are read immediately after the opening ceremonies at the first meeting of each day.

20.41 Business unfinished at the end of a day is normally taken up after the reading of the minutes, provided that there is no conflict with a special order.

20.42 Nominations and elections should take place relatively early in the convention so that there will be time to complete balloting if more than one ballot must be taken.

Arrangements Committee

20.43 An arrangements committee is concerned with physical arrangements, such as a place to meet, hotel accommodations, and other related services. This committee is largely made up of members from a constituent unit acting as the convention hosts. It should include individuals with prior experience in conventions.

20.44 The principal duties of the arrangements committee, some of which may be delegated to subcommittees or distributed among several committees, are as follows:

- Selecting convention headquarters
- Arranging room accommodations
- Meeting dignitaries and honored guests at the airport or rail station
- Producing printed material giving directions for getting to the convention by all available types of transportation

- Determining seating arrangements in the assembly hall
- Arranging for pages, ushers, doorkeepers, and the like
- Liaison with the program committee to insure proper seating on the platform
- Arranging for proper staffing of the information desk
- Arranging for local media to cover important happenings, insuring the availability of typewriters, copiers, telephones, telegraph, and other systems of communication.

Resolutions Committee

20.45 The resolutions committee screens all original main motions that are to come before the convention.

20.46 Depending on its size, structure, and other factors peculiar to itself, each organization decides the best method to be used in presenting resolutions to the delegates of its constituent units when they assemble for a convention. This decision becomes the basis from which permanent rules are developed and placed in the bylaws. Some organizations permit the offering of a resolution directly from the floor of the convention, others require that all resolutions be submitted a specified number of days, weeks, or even months before the convention. In this latter case of prior submission, provisions should also be made to permit the introduction of a resolution directly to the delegates of the convention provided that body, by a two-thirds vote, will permit its introduction.

20.47 Bylaws can prescribe any number of ways in which resolutions can be introduced to the delegates of the convention. For example, they may allow resolutions to be introduced by any member of the organization, only by a delegate, by a delegate or other voting members of the convention who have been registered, through the sponsorship of a constituent unit, or by standing or special committees of the organization. All of these are usually subject to the screening process of the resolutions committee as are the recommendations of the officers of the organization, which are reworded into proper resolutions before being presented to the delegates.

20.48 In some organizations the resolutions committee originates and drafts its own resolutions. One of its principal duties is to draft courtesy resolutions lauding the accomplishments of outstanding individuals whose actions reflect great credit on the organization, or to express thanks to those whose assistance helped to ensure the success of the convention. The chair, in putting the question on courtesy resolutions to vote, puts only the affirmative part of the question before the assembly, never the negative, unless someone objects.

20.49 Resolutions committees, unless authorized by the bylaws or convention standing rules, are unable to take any action other than to transform recommendations received into resolutions, to put resolutions into proper form, and to eliminate duplications before reporting all resolutions to the delegates of the convention. Some committees are authorized to make substantive changes in a resolution but only with the approval of the sponsor. Others are empowered to make changes, even to completely alter the substance of a referred resolution, without obtaining consent. A committee granted this authority, should impose upon itself a requirement of at least a two-thirds vote before taking such action.

20.50 Unless the bylaws provide otherwise, the resolutions committee must report all resolutions referred to it. The committee does have the right to recommend to the assembly on any resolution which is reported, either that the resolution be adopted or be *not* adopted. If the committee is uncertain or would prefer to remain uncommitted when presenting the resolution to the assembled delegates, the reporting member, after making the report, would simply state, "no recommendation."

Some organizations' bylaws give the resolutions committee the right *not* to report. This usually stems from the need of the assembly to transact a large amount of business in a short period of time. Whatever the reason, any committee having the power to withhold a resolution from consideration by the assembly should have built in controls such as an extremely high vote of the committee before it can exercise such a prerogative. (RONR suggests a three-fourths vote or a vote of two-thirds of the membership of the entire committee.) In addition, the bylaws should prescribe that the assembly by a majority vote, can overturn the decision of the committee and order it to report the resolution.

20.51 The report of the resolutions committee follows the procedure of any committee reporting on a resolution referred to it. It is not necessary to "move to adopt" unless the committee itself originates the resolution. Resolutions are always treated as if they had been moved and seconded when reported to the assembly by the resolutions committee. It is possible for a committee to propose an amendment to a referred resolution, then recommend that the resolution as amended be adopted. In an instance of this kind the motion to "adopt the amendment" is in order. "By direction of the committee, I move to adopt the proposed amendment and that the resolution, as thus amended, be adopted."

Glossary

Abstain. Refrain from voting on the question.

Ad hoc. For this special purpose. (Latin term.)

Adjourn. To officially close a meeting.

Adjourned meeting. Continuation of the meeting at which the motion for an adjourned meeting was made.

Adjourn sine die. Close a meeting with no plans for a future meeting. (Latin term.)

Adopt. To accept, approve, agree to, or to ratify.

Affirmative vote. Favorable vote for the question, usually by a show of hands in a small assembly or a rising vote in a large assembly.

Agenda. A detailed listing of the items in the order of business for a specific meeting.

Alternate. A member authorized to replace, if needed, a legally named delegate to a convention.

Amend. To modify or change the wording of a pending question provided the question is amendable according to the rules governing.

Assembly. Members of an organization who have assembled to transact business.

Audit. An examination and verification of financial accounts and records of an organization.

Ballot. A secret vote, usually written.

Board. Members of an organization elected and authorized to transact business for the organization within certain limitations as prescribed in the bylaws.

Business. Matters to be considered by the assembly, usually termed the agenda in the order of business.

Bylaws. Contain the basic rules adopted by the organization, which prescribe how the organization shall conduct its internal affairs.

Candidate. One who seeks office.

Chairman. One who presides at a board meeting, a committee meeting, or the meeting of an assembly.

Chairman pro tem. A temporary chairman, elected or appointed to preside during the absence of the regular chairman.

Convention. A formal assembly of delegates who are usually chosen for one session only.

Courtesy resolution. A resolution expressing thanks for assistance or commending meritorious accomplishments.

Credential. Written evidence of entitlement to be a delegate or alternate to a convention.

Debatable. A question that may be discussed under the rules of debate.

Debate. A discussion of a question in an assembly in which the affirmative and negative sides are advocated by opposing speakers.

Decorum. Conduct of an orderly nature in keeping with recognized standards of social behavior during meetings of an assembly.

Delegate. The official representative of a constituent unit of an organization who is authorized to attend and take part in the organization's convention.

Deliberative assembly. Usually a smaller group of members of an organization meeting together with authority to transact business in the name of the entire organization.

Division of the Assembly. A demand that the vote be retaken as a rising vote. (Sometimes the shortened term "Division" is used.)

Division of the Question. A motion to separate a pending question into two or more distinct parts so that each can be debated and voted upon separately.

Executive board. *See* Board.

Executive session. A meeting in which the proceedings are secret and only members or others who are specially invited may attend.

Ex officio. By virtue of official position.

Fiscal year. Yearly period in which an organization determines its financial condition without regard to calendar year.

Fix the Time to Which to Adjourn. A motion designating time and place for a continuation of the current meeting which must be held before the next regular meeting.

Floor, to obtain. When a member is recognized by the presiding officer so that he/she alone is authorized to speak, that member is said to have "obtained the floor."

General consent. Silent consent. The adoption of a motion without a vote being taken when it appears that everyone is in agreement.

General Orders. Items of business which are placed in the agenda as orders of the day to be taken up following unfinished business, usually in the sequential order in which they were made.

Germane. Relevant and appropriate, as a primary amendment is in its relationship to the pending question or a secondary amendment is in its relationship to a primary amendment.

Illegal vote. A vote not credited to any party, but one that is counted as a part of the total number of votes cast, which is the number used in computing a majority.

Immediately Pending Question. The last motion stated by the chair that has not been voted upon.

Incidental Main Motion. A main motion which relates to

the business of the assmbly, usually used to ratify or change some past action or to propose some future action.

Incidental Motion. A motion that arises out of a question being considered or one that relates to the business of the assembly. It must be disposed of before further action can be taken on the pending question or other business.

Indecorum. Improper or disorderly conduct, disruptive to the orderly proceedings of the assembly.

Informal consideration. A method of considering a question without observing all the rules of formal debate.

Main motion. A main motion brings before the assembly a subject for consideration and action.

Majority vote. More than half the votes cast by members entitled to vote.

Mass meeting. A meeting usually open to anyone in sympathy with the purpose of the meeting as defined by the sponsors.

Minority vote. Less than half the vote cast by members entitled to vote.

Nomination. The formal naming of a person who is being recommended for appointment or election to office.

Nominee. A person who has been nominated for office.

Order of business. Schedule of business in a formal program with items arranged in the order in which they are to be considered by an assembly in a specific meeting.

Original main motion. Introduces a new subject to the assembly.

Out of order. Not in keeping with the rules of the organization.

Parliamentary inquiry. A request for information regarding proper parliamentary procedure.

Pending question. A motion that has been stated by the chair but has not been put to vote.

Personal privilege. Concerns the right of a member to be protected against disorder, annoyance, or discomfort.

Plurality vote. The largest number of votes received when there are at least three choices.

Point of order. An incidental motion calling attention to a violation of parliamentary rules.

Preamble. An introduction preceding a resolution, stating the reason for its proposal.

Precedence. (Pronounced pre ce' dence.) The rank of motions, which establishes the order in which they are to be acted upon.

Prevailing side. The winning side.

Previous question. A motion whose adoption stops debate and amendments to the pending question(s).

Primary amendment. The first amendment to the main motion, sometimes called an amendment of the first degree.

Privileged motion. A motion of such high importance that it can interrrupt the assembly's business.

Program. An all inclusive list of activities for a given session, such as times for speakers, meals, entertainment, and other activities of a non-business nature as opposed to "Agenda," which technically includes only items of business.

Pro tem. *(Pro tempore.)* Latin term meaning temporarily; for the time being.

Putting the question. The chair formally places the question before the assembly to allow members to express their collective opinion by vote.

Question. A motion, after being stated by the chair, becomes a question that introduces a matter to the assembly for necessary action.

Question of privilege. A privileged motion requesting permission to make a motion or a request affecting the rights of the assembly or any of its members.

Quorum. Number of members required to be present at a business meeting before business can be conducted legally. The quorum is always a majority of all members unless stated otherwise in the bylaws.

Rank. Rank and precedence are synonymous terms. *See* Precedence.

Ratify. To legally approve action previously taken without a quorum being present or an emergency action taken under unusual circumstances. An assembly can ratify only such action as it would have the right to authorize.

Receive a report. A report is received as soon as it is heard by the assembly. No motion is necessary to "receive the report."

Recess. Short intermission taken by the assembly during a meeting.

Recognition. The chair formally acknowledges a member thus giving the member entitlement to the floor and the right to speak.

Recommit. To refer a matter reported by a committee back to that committee.

Reconsider. To consider for a second time the vote on a question that was previously adopted or defeated.

Reconsider and Enter on the Minutes. A motion which, if made, prevents reconsideration of the vote on the motion to which it applies on the same day the vote was taken.

Rescind. To annual previous action or to strike out an entire resolution previously adopted.

Resolution. A formal written motion, which may include a preamble giving the reasons for making the motion. Each enacting clause of the resolution normally begins with the word "Resolved" although an alternate form may be used.

Revision of bylaws. Presenting a completely new set of bylaws to the organization for approval as opposed to amendment of extant bylaws.

Rules of order. Rules contained in the adopted parliamentary authority of an organization are the organization's rules of order.

Ruling. An official decision of the presiding officer on a parliamentary matter that is before the assembly.

Secondary amendment. A secondary amendment is an amendment to an amendment. It is also called an amendment of the second degree.

Secondary motion. A generalized term which can apply to any subsidiary, privileged, or incidental motion.

Seconding a motion. A member, other than the maker of the motion, indicates by saying, "Second" or "I second the motion" that he/she is in favor of having the motion considered by the assembly.

Seriatim. In a series; one after another. In parliamentary terminology it means to consider a given document by paragraphs or by sections.

Session. A session can terminate at the end of a single meeting, or can last through a series of connected meetings as in a convention.

Sine die. Latin term meaning "without day." When an assembly adjourns sine die it is dissolved, and that assembly ceases to exist.

Special committee. A special (ad hoc) committee is brought into being to accomplish a specific task. It automatically ceases to exist when the job is done.

Special meeting. A meeting called for a specific purpose as expressed in the call for the meeting.

Special order. A motion or subject assigned a certain time in the agenda. When that time arrives it interrupts any pending business except consideration of another special order made before it was made.

Standing committees. Permanent committees that exist throughout the life of the organization that establishes them.

Standing rules. Standing rules of an organization (not to be confused with convention standing rules) are rules that relate to the details of administration rather than to parliamentary procedure.

Stating the question. The chair restates the motion after it is moved and seconded. This formally places the question before the assembly for whatever action it chooses to take.

Subsidiary motion. A motion belonging to a class of motions that modifies, delays action, or disposes of the main motion.

Substitute amendment. A form of an amendment which proposes to strike out an entire resolution or a paragraph and insert another in its place. The substitute must be germane to the pending question but can be hostile.

Suspend the rules. An incidental motion that permits the assembly to temporarily set aside the regular rules in order to accomplish a specific purpose. Fundamental rules of the bylaws cannot be suspended.

Sustain the chair. Uphold a ruling of the chair.

Table a motion. To lay a motion aside temporarily so that more urgent business can be taken up. This motion is never qualified as to the length of time the motion to which it is applied shall remain on the table.

Take from the table. When in order—that is, during business of the same class, or unfinished or new business—this motion takes precedence over any main motion made but not stated by the chair. When a question is taken from the table, it is returned to the assembly in the same condition as it was before being laid on the table.

Tellers. The chair usually appoints the tellers to count the ballots of a vote. No one should be allowed in the room where the ballots are being counted except the tellers.

Two-thirds vote. Two-thirds of the votes cast by members legally entitled to vote.

Unanimous consent. *See* General consent.

Undebatable motion. A motion which, under the rules of parliamentary law, cannot be debated.

Unfinished business. Items of business not completed at the previous meeting.

Vacating the chair. The presiding officer relinquishes the chair; usually to participate in the debate of a substantive matter.

Viva voce vote. A voice vote.

Withdraw a motion. Maker may withdraw a motion before

it is stated by the chair. After being stated by the chair, permission must be obtained from the assembly to withdraw the motion.

Yield. To relinquish or to give way to something. A motion yields to the precedence of another motion.

Yielding the floor. To voluntarily release one's time to another speaker.

Index